CARING FOR YOUR CHERISHED POSSESSIONS

CARING FOR YOUR CHERISHED POSSESSIONS

The Experts' Guide to Cleaning, Preserving, and
Protecting Your China, Silver, Furniture, Clothing,
Paintings, and More

Mary Kerney Levenstein
Cordelia Frances Biddle

Illustrations by Lauren Jarrett

Crown Publishers, Inc.
New York

Published by Crown Publishers, Inc., 201 East 50th Street, New York, New York 10022

CROWN is a trademark of Crown Publishers, Inc.
Manufactured in the United States of America

Library of Congress Cataloging-in-Publication Data

Levenstein, Mary Kerney.
Caring for your cherished possessions
The Experts' Guide to Cleaning, Preserving, and Protecting Your China, Silver, Furniture, Clothing, Paintings, and More / Mary Kerney Levenstein, Cordelia Frances Biddle.
p.   cm.
Bibliography: p.
Includes index.
1. House furnishings—Conservation and restoration.   2. Clothing—Conservation and restoration.   3. House furnishings—Cleaning.
4. Clothing—Cleaning.   I. Biddle, Cordelia Frances.   II. Title.
TX323.L48   1989
643—dc19   89-653
ISBN 0-517-57087-4
10   9   8   7   6   5   4   3   2   1
First Edition

Contents

■

*F*oreword

■

How many times have we wondered, "What *is* the proper way to care for this special possession?" Well, hooray, for now we have the answer to almost every such conceivable question included in this informative and highly readable book.

Did you know, for instance, that your favorite wool sweater may have acid in its makeup? Yes, acid. Well, it may, and when you store it you should do so in buffered tissue with an alkaline Ph factor.

Or that your carpets can actually become brittle—as well as grow mold?

Or that certain furniture should be vacuumed instead of simply dusted?

That chemicals in ordinary tap water can damage bronze and other metal pots and vases?

Or that certain pottery shouldn't be immersed in water because it will actually swell?

That you shouldn't worry about that odd moth flying around? Why? Because the moth is not the problem; the problem is its eggs that have already been laid.

Well, I didn't, and I marvel at the research and the solutions that the authors reveal, including new products and state-of-the-art techniques to clean, restore, and preserve our treasured belongings.

This book will help you learn to take care of your fancy wedding dress and antique lace, your patchwork quilts and wicker baskets, your treasured photograph albums, your paintings, and your antique furniture, so that you will be able to enjoy the things you love for years to come.

Because it covers virtually everything we have in our homes, this is an indispensable guide for every household. Additionally and most importantly, it includes a separate chapter listing resources and experts across the country to call upon for advice.

This is a book we have all needed for many years.

CHARLOTTE FORD

Preface

This guide is for people who own fine things and want to know how to take care of them. In looking for ways to clean, protect, and preserve the contents of our own homes, it has become clear to us that we and most people have been treating valued possessions improperly. Until now, the most current, detailed, and thoroughly reliable information has been immediately available only to conservators and restorers.

In our research we found that many factors have changed and modern technology has had to respond to atmospheric pollutants and contaminants in today's environment. Some cleaning techniques that date back several generations are still considered the best. At the same time, we learned that there are new techniques and new barrier products available to protect and preserve vulnerable art objects, furnishings, and textiles.

We found too that new evaluative processes provide us with a better approach to treatment. For example, many museums now have access to textile scanners that reveal fiber content, detect age, and identify the elements to which the fabric has been exposed.

In our effort to provide the most authoritative information on both preservation, which prevents or retards deterioration, and restoration, which reverses it, we have interviewed conservators, restorers, collectors, and master craftsmen who are experts in their fields.

We have presented their knowledge in a readily accessible fashion. We hope that as a result of our sharing this information we will enable many a thing of beauty to remain a joy forever.

*L*inens and Clothing

■

A hundred years ago a favored remedy for scorched clothing consisted of a paste of vinegar, fuller's earth, soap, onion juice, and fowl's dung. This was spread on the burned garment and allowed to dry, then the garment was washed twice with the hope that it would come completely clean. Fortunately, most such old recipes have been replaced. Clothing and linens can now be treated and preserved with more knowledgeable and informed care.

To protect fine textiles, it is important, first of all, to clean and store them properly. No wedding dress, no table linens, no antique lace, no newly dry-cleaned evening dress, *nothing* should ever be stored in plastic. Plastic prevents air circulation. Trapped beneath it, the fabric cannot breathe, fibers begin to break down, and eventually they disintegrate. Buttons, beads, and sequins fall off as the cotton thread securing them rots. The sequins themselves discolor, and if they are made of organic material they will finally crumble.

Storage

Clothing should be hung in muslin clothing bags or under a pure cotton sheet draped over the closet rod. Position the sheet over the hangers to hang to the floor on each side. This keeps out dust, dirt, and light, but allows the movement of air and prevents dampness. Hang especially valued clothing in bags made of barrier materials such as Gore-Tex™. This acid-free product is breathable, but keeps out water, dust, mold spores, bacteria, and smoke.

Leave space between clothes on the rod. Hang heavy garments, such as beaded blouses, on padded hangers, which distribute weight and stress. Men's suits require formed wooden hangers that are wide enough to support the shoulders.

Store special dresses that are very heavy or old and knits or clothing not often worn in special archival boxes. These boxes are made of acid-free material and have no pastes or oils to stain delicate materials. Before carefully folding garments, stuff them with acid-free tissue so that their shape is maintained.

The fibers in textiles can break if they remain folded flat for a long time. The crease line stresses the fabric, and as the fabric deteriorates along the line, tears develop. Fabric also discolors along the fold, both in clothing and linens.

Weight causes fold lines to set, so don't store too many heavy garments on top of each other in one box. A separate box for each stored item and plenty of layers of acid-free tissue along folds assure you that a wedding dress or lace tablecloth will be just as lovely twenty years from now as it is today. Periodically remove and refold clothing along new lines.

Wool, cotton, and linen fabrics often have an acid content and should be stored in buffered tissue with an alkaline pH factor. Store silks in neutral or unbuffered paper. The pH scale, from 0 to 14, expresses the degree of alkalinity or acidity. A factor of 7 is neutral. Lower factors have more hydrogen ions and are acidic, higher are alkaline. Each degree differs from the next by a factor of 10, so a pH of 3 is 10 times more concentrated than a pH of 4 and 100 times more than a pH of 5.

Before storing table or bed linens, wash and rinse them in soft water. Hard water leaves a residue of iron, which over time rusts and leaves brown spots. To test for hardness, put one pint of hot water from your faucet and one teaspoon of laundry detergent into a one-quart jar. Shake vigorously. If it becomes very sudsy and remains so for several minutes, the water is soft. If there are no suds or if bubbles break up quickly, you should add a laundry water softener to your wash. Many laundry detergents already contain water softeners, sometimes identified as sodium carbonate (washing soda, sal soda, or soda ash) or phosphates, so read their labels. Before storing extremely old or valuable textiles, wash them in distilled or demineralized water, which is free from all stain-causing properties.

No linens should be sized or starched if you plan to leave them stored for any length of time. Sizing and starch are corrosive and should be used for articles that will be used and rewashed in the foreseeable future. When storing in cardboard, metal, or wooden boxes or drawers, be sure to cover surfaces with plenty of acid-free tissue or a barrier product such as Gore-Tex to prevent the migration of deteriorating agents to fabric.

Avoid potpourri, lavender, or any other sachets in storage. The oil from these dried flowers can eat away at fine fabrics and in time you may find your lovely table mats full of holes. Save sachets for your lingerie drawer or for clothing that is rotated, washed, and aired with some frequency.

Moths and Insect Pests

■

Don't lose sleep over moths you see flying around your house. By the time they are fluttering about your lamps and window screens, their eggs are laid, and it's these larvae that do the damage. In fact, moth larvae damage more clothing and home furnishings in the United States each year than fire does.

Wool, fur, feathers, and dog and cat hair are favorite haunts of moths and other insect pests. They nest in dark, quiet places: in closets, around baseboards, under radiators, behind curtains, and beneath the folded edges of wall-to-wall carpets. Do not carpet closet floors. Dirt that falls into the carpet pile and lack of light combine to create an irresistible breeding ground.

Cedar or lavender, because of their strong odor, are excellent moth deterrents and are nontoxic. Lavender may be placed near stored articles but not touching them since the oils will damage textile fibers. However, these are deterrents, and they will not kill larvae already present on clothes placed in storage.

Dimethyldichlorovinylphosphate (DDVP) and paradichlorobenzene (PDB) are two effective and widely available chemicals that kill infesting insects. DDVP is sold in hanging no-pest strips. PDB, sold as paranuggets or paracrystals, is more effective than crystals labeled naphthalene, because naphthalene controls moths but does not kill crickets, carpet beetles, water bugs, silverfish, cockroaches, or a variety of other insect pests. The carpet beetle, or buffalo moth, eats faster than the clothes moth and is far more ruinous. It feasts on carpet pile and upholstery as well as on clothing. Other insects infest clothing and linens without devouring the fibers, but the resultant soil and stains can be irreversible.*

---

* Certain substances used to clean and protect linens and clothing are highly toxic and many have been linked to cancer. They include DDVP, PDB, and naphthalene, used to control moths; phenol, used for mildew control; formaldehyde; chlorine bleach; Lestoil ™ and similar products;

Hang no-pest strips (DDVP) or paracrystals (PDB) as high as possible, because the vapors are heavier than air. When clothes are removed from storage, air them in a well-ventilated area. Read and follow label instructions with extreme care because these chemicals are highly toxic.

When storing folded articles, spread paracrystals or nuggets between each layer. Vacuum weekly and clean and air dark or remote places thoroughly and regularly. Keep a few paranuggets in your vacuum bag. Call your state department of agriculture to find out what period of the year is considered moth season in your area and during these months empty vacuum bags after each use.

Many infesting insects, especially moths, like and thrive on grease, so nothing should be stored unless completely free of grease and stains.

Moth infestation must be treated immediately. All clothing in the house should be inspected. Throw away what cannot be salvaged. Dry-clean all woolens, furs, feathers, and any other articles in which you see holes or on which you see white moth larvae. Notify the cleaner that moth infestation is present.

While infested items are at the cleaners, have the house exterminated for moths and preferably mothproofed. Ask for a guarantee when contracting for this service. A good exterminator or mothproofing expert will be alert to the possible presence of a moth nest in such an unlikely place as a radiator pipe. Be sure to get specific instructions regarding whether you should leave the house, and for how long, when extermination is in progress.

Before returning cleaned clothing to the house, dampen a cloth with water and wipe off shoes, boxes, gloves, and everything else in closets or areas where the infestation occurred. Throw out the cloth.

If your house has been infested, protect storage areas conscientiously and inspect regularly for signs of reinfestation. Insect larvae may remain alive in a dormant state for several years.

hydrofluoric and oxalic acids, used to remove rust stains; and dry-cleaning solvents (benzene, toluene, trichloroethylene, and perchloroethylene). Always wear rubber gloves when using these materials, and do not inhale their fumes. Dispose of products and containers as hazardous waste.

*M*ildew

■

To prevent mildew, keep linens, clothing, and storage areas well ventilated, dry, and clean. Grease and dirt provide food for mildew spores. In damp climates leave a small electric bulb burning continuously in each closet. This provides enough heat to retard mildew. Cover textiles to avoid overexposure to light.

Mildew prevention is easier than mildew removal. Sometimes treatment is impossible and odor and black spots are there to stay. Vapors from hanging paracrystals and cloth bags of paraformaldehyde inhibit mildew growth. Hang these in damp closets or other areas where a mildew problem is present or anticipated. Spray damp areas and mist fabrics with Lysol Spray™, which is orthophenylphenol in ethanol. Don't use liquid Lysol, which is a different formulation.

If you find mildew, act quickly. Thoroughly brush or vacuum mildew stains outdoors to avoid scattering spores (seeds) in the house. Pour strong soap and salt on the spots and place in the sunlight. Then wash the mildewed article in borax and water. If this is not strong enough to remove stains, apply the following solution with a soft brush: ¼ teaspoon of peroxy (all-fabric) bleach, or detergent containing sodium perborate, dissolved in ¼ cup of fresh (newly opened) 3 percent hydrogen peroxide. Hydrogen peroxide that has been stored in an opened bottle for a prolonged period won't work. After ten minutes, wipe dry with a clean cloth until the stain is no longer present.

Launder washable articles in hot sudsy water and, if possible, dry them in the sun. Send nonwashable articles to the dry cleaner right away.

In the nineteenth century, mildewed articles were dipped in sour buttermilk, spread in the sun to dry, and then rinsed in clear water. This is still often effective and is certainly worth a try if spots and odor prove persistent. Buttermilk is a cultured milk product and sours approximately three to six weeks after the printed expiration date on the carton. It will be clear to you when it has turned, by either smell or taste.

*D*ry Cleaning

Many people take clothes to the dry cleaner for cleaning when they merely need pressing. Most cleaners are willing to press without cleaning. When your clothes are clean but rumpled, ask for this service. It is almost impossible to press certain garments at home and achieve the same result a professional does. But never press or have pressed any article that is stained or dirty. The iron's heat will set the stains and trap the dirt.

Dry cleaning is appropriate for heavy wools, tweeds, gabardines, velvets, metallic fabrics, some silks and satins, and much of the contemporary wardrobe. Dry-clean sparingly. The fluids and chemicals used can abrade, scratch, and bruise delicate textile fibers. Vibration of the dry-cleaning drum can stress fabrics, especially vintage clothing already weakened by age, and heat used in the process can shrink or felt (mat) some materials.

Dry cleaning by hand with fresh solvents is available at some cleaners and, though more expensive, is desirable for fragile, valued clothing.

*W*ashing

Fortunately, there are a number of simply formulated wash products to replace more elaborate mixtures, such as that recommended in 1859 to

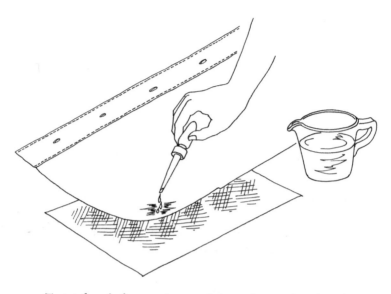

*To test for colorfastness, let several drops of water drip through
an inside seam of the fabric onto a cloth or paper blotter placed underneath
to see if color seeps through.*

■

wash silk: one half-pint of gin, one half-pound each of honey and soft
soap, and one half-pint of water.

As with all products, read and follow label directions when using
soaps, detergents, surfactants (which penetrate fabrics and/or lift off
stains). Washable woolens should be hand-washed and if necessary
soaked in a mild soap such as Ivory Flakes™, Ensure™, or Fels
Naptha™. Pure soaps are natural fatty products that won't work or
dissolve in cold water, so keep the water tepid. Regular laundry
products often work well in cold water, but should be used only in very
small amounts for washing by hand, because they contain sodium
carbonates (water softeners) and other ingredients that are corrosive in
dense concentrations. Use special cold-water wash products according
to label instructions, and don't let fabrics soak longer than three

minutes. These products are detergents and are not as mild as the mildest soaps.

Don't wash sweaters by hand if they are embroidered, Fair Isle design, or of a tightly twisted pattern. Washing may run the colors of embroidery or Fair Isle designs or mat the twisted patterns.

To test any article for colorfastness before washing, use an inside seam. Place a white cloth or blotter under the test area, let several drops of distilled water fall onto the material, and check the blotter to see whether the color has seeped through. If the article fails the test, consider soaking it in white vinegar and hot water to set the dye. Rinse well, dry, then test again. White vinegar is safe for all fibers, but may occasionally change some dye colors. If this begins to happen, immediately neutralize the vinegar with a solution of one tablespoon of ammonia and one cup of water.

Wash cotton, washable silk, synthetic, and linen fabrics that are old or delicate as above. Some of the new rayons and viscose rayons may be washed according to label directions, but it is safer to dry-clean old rayons, or they may shrink several sizes, usually unevenly. Don't wash wrinkle-resistant fabrics in very hot water or dry them with prolonged high heat or they may lose some of their permanent-press properties.

A washing product used by museum curators and textile restorers, and recommended for all fine fabrics except silk, is Orvis WA Paste™. Thorough rinsing with this and with all wash products is critical. Soap remaining after washing becomes sticky, attracts dust, and, if ironed, will scorch.

S tarching

■

To achieve the crisp and resilient finish that new cotton and linen fabrics lose in laundering, use a laundry starch. Cornstarch is the basic ingredient in these products, and there is a good deal more of it in powders than in liquids. Be sure that a starch solution is very hot when clean clothes are immersed, and you will avoid the shiny spots that result from uneven distribution.

To stiffen delicate organdies and batistes you may substitute a solution of one packet of unflavored gelatin dissolved in four pints of hot water. Before ironing starched clothes, sprinkle them with warm water, even when using a steam iron.

Among spray products, sizing is as effective as and less harsh than some of the spray starches.

Bleaching

Bleaches are either chlorine based or peroxy. Peroxy bleaches contain sodium perborate with an alkali such as sodium carbonate (washing soda, sal soda, or soda ash).

Textile conservators are reluctant to recommend bleach because it is highly corrosive. Their business is textile preservation and not usage; ours is both. Whether or not to subject very old and delicate laces and cottons to bleach can be a difficult decision, not undertaken without a degree of risk.

Anyone who has ever overbleached a blouse or other article of clothing, and lifted it out of the bleach water in shreds, knows how potent an overdose can be.

The mildest whitening solution consists of 1½ gallons of cold water and one cup of peroxy (all-fabric) bleach. A homemade peroxy bleach is three parts bleaching hydrogen peroxide to one part ammonia. If using a powdered peroxy bleach, dissolve it first in a small amount of very hot water. Soak the garment for two hours, checking periodically.

These bleaches are nonchlorine and slow-acting.

A stronger solution is ¼ to one cup of sodium hexametaphosphate per five gallons of water. This is a nontoxic chlorine bleach substitute. Soak articles until white, usually an hour or more.

A still stronger recipe is two gallons of water and ½ cup of liquid chlorine bleach. This is fast-acting and, depending on the fabric, may whiten in only ten to twenty minutes. If not, keep soaking, checking frequently, and after four hours change the water and add fresh bleach, increasing the amount slightly if desired.

For a very strong solution, add one cup of dishwashing detergent to the above. This is risky and should be saved for last-ditch efforts, when the alternative is to relegate the item to the rag pile.

Never mix chlorine bleach with ammonia or products containing ammonia. The chemical combination produces chloramines, whose fumes can be fatal.

The most traditional method of whitening clothes and keeping them white is exposure to sunlight. Try this for summer whites, for Edwardian, Victorian, or vintage whites, and for delicate laces and linens. Hang clothing on a clean clothesline or spread it on a clean sheet on dry ground. Don't bring it in until the sun goes down. Better yet, if you are an early riser, spread clothing on the ground directly on dewy grass. Among dew's legendary, magical properties, whitening is one of the foremost.

*P*ressing

■

Pressing is an art, and a handful of special professionals are so adept at it that they are in demand by museums, film and television productions, haute couture designers, and mothers of the bride. For the rest of us, ironing is a chore made a good deal easier and pleasanter with proper equipment and methods.

In addition to your board and iron, you need a sleeveboard and a device known as a "ham," which is held by a handgrip and stuffed into padded shoulders with one hand while the other steams or presses. You might also want a device to hold pleats in place. Run the iron over a block of wax to make it glide faster, and follow heat settings diligently.

Before pressing a difficult garment, study it as you would a map: its grain, its seams, its ruffles. There is a logical starting point and progression. Don't rush. Ironing requires time and patience.

If the garment is long, spread a clean sheet on the floor under the board. Iron everything possible on the wrong side to avoid shine spots. Touch up on the right side, using a pressing cloth if necessary. Always press embroidery or lace on the back to keep the stitching raised.

Start a dress at the neck. Then do the sleeves, the back and front, and work down the skirt. When sleeves are finished, stuff them with tissue. Start a shirt at the yoke, then progress to the collar, cuffs, sleeves, front, and back, in sequence. Avoid bumpy collars by starting at each end of the collar and ironing into the middle. Start pants with the pockets, then the inside waistband, the zipper and its side panels, the seat, and last, with a pressing cloth, do the legs.

Use a folded towel, an old blanket, or a piece of flannel under laces and delicate materials. To keep the folded edges of neckties soft, insert a piece of cardboard cut to size, then press.

Always iron with the grain to avoid misshaping. This levels the hems of bias-cut garments, which sometimes become uneven after washing. It also keeps seams straight and aligns the sides and corners of square cloths or napkins. When ironing garments that are cut on the bias or have panel inserts, be careful to flatten but not to pull the cloth. Velvet simply cannot be ironed without a metal attachment that keeps the pile standing, so don't court disaster by trying.

To pack pressed clothing, stuff it with lots of tissue. If you have saved the dry cleaner's plastic bags, use them as you would tissue, and save the brown paper wrapping from laundered shirts to stuff the sleeves and shoulders of heavy jackets. Pack bags firmly but not to bursting, and if possible carry an extra small bag just for heavy items such as shoes, cosmetics, books, tapes, and cameras. Your clothing will emerge as freshly pressed as when it was packed.

Stain Removal

Washable Cotton, Synthetic, and Linen Fabrics

■

When attempting to treat a stain, remember that you are proceeding at your own risk and not all stains can be removed. If possible, start treatment right away. Stains are much more difficult to remove once they have set.

Stains are greasy, nongreasy, or a combination of both. Basic treatment is as follows:

Greasy stains, such as butter, cheese, chocolate, crayon, eyeliner, and lipstick: Presoak for five to ten minutes in Lestoil, a presoak product such as Shout™ or Spray 'N Wash™, or Murphy Oil Soap™. Launder cold. If any trace of the stain remains, soak eight hours or overnight in one gallon of cold water and ½ cup of peroxy (all-fabric) bleach. If the bleach is powdered, dissolve it in hot water first, then add to cold water. Heat sets stains. Don't wash with hot water, iron, or machine-dry on a heat setting until every trace of the stain is gone.

If you are unable to treat a grease stain quickly, sprinkle it liberally with salt, which is an absorbent. This is a favorite trick of actors, who often find themselves on tour without time to find a good dry cleaner between performances or before leaving town. Other equally effective absorbents are cornmeal, cornstarch, French chalk, and fuller's earth.

Nongreasy stains, such as berries, coffee, fruit, tomatoes, and wine: Neutralize by soaking in cool water, which has a pH factor of 7. Then proceed as above.

The following stains on washable white and colorfast fabrics have been removed this way. (Use Lestoil only on colorfast cotton, synthetic, and linen fabric, not on washable woolens and silk.)

alcoholic beverages	grease
antiperspirant	jam
berries	jelly
blood	ketchup
blush powder	lipstick
butter	mascara
cheese	mustard
chocolate	paprika
cider vinegar	pencil
cocoa	perfume
coffee	shoe polish
crayon	soft drinks
deodorant	suntan oil
eyeliner	tomato
felt-tip pen	wine
fruit	wine vinegar
grass	

Combination stains, such as cream and coffee: treat as nongreasy, then as greasy, following the steps above.

There are several other common stains for which this process doesn't work. Treat them as follows:

Ballpoint ink. Using an absorbent layer of material underneath, soak with denatured or rubbing alcohol. Apply lukewarm or room-temperature glycerin, then flush with water. Apply several drops of

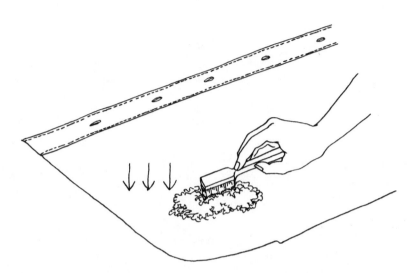

*To tamp a stain, tap a soft nylon-bristle toothbrush
on it firmly and squarely, repeating the motion swiftly, to cause
stain-removing agents to penetrate the fabric.*

■

ammonia and flush quickly with water again. Within minutes, ammonia may have an alkaline effect on dyes, changing their color and requiring neutralization with white vinegar. Work quickly and flush thoroughly to prevent this from happening. If the fabric is strong enough, use a soft nylon-bristle toothbrush, preferably an old one, to tamp the stain at each stage. To tamp, place the brush on the stain lightly but squarely and firmly, and repeat this motion until no stain is evident. Natural bristles become soft when wet and won't do as effective a job. For persistent ballpoint ink stains, sponge with milk and white vinegar, and repeat the process until they disappear.

Candle wax. Place the stained fabric between layers of absorbent paper and iron at low temperature. As the paper absorbs the wax, change it, until no more wax melts. If any stain remains, apply a solution of one tablespoon of water and chlorine bleach on white, or peroxy (all-fabric) bleach on colors, and flush immediately with water once again. Candles won't drip if frozen for twenty-four hours before lighting.

Chewing gum. Rub with ice. Gum will flake off.

Perspiration. Sponge with water, then with detergent and water. If the stain is fresh, sponge next with ammonia. If the fabric is fragile, pass the stained area over the mouth of the ammonia bottle to bring it into contact with the fumes. If the stain is old, sponge it with white vinegar. Rinse. If oily traces remain after drying, sponge with dry-cleaning solvent, but solvent won't work on the stain itself, which must be dissolved with water. If odor remains after washing, soak for an hour or more in one tablespoon of salt per quart of water. A simple and effective way to avoid perspiration stains is always to use dress shields.

Pet urine stains. Apply one ounce of ammonia mixed with eight ounces of cold water. Pour the mixture on and leave it until the bubbling stops. Then sponge it with fresh water and white vinegar.

Rust. Dampen with water and apply a few drops of Whink™, which is hydrofluoric acid. The stain will be gone in seconds. Neutralize immediately by rinsing well with water. Don't iron before rinsing completely. Oxalic acid may be used the same way. If these products aren't on hand, try lemon juice, or boil the stained article in one pint of water and four teaspoons of cream of tartar, and rinse well.

Scorch. Apply detergent directly to the scorch mark and wash normally. If the scorch remains, wet it with cool water and apply a solution of hydrogen peroxide and a few drops of ammonia. Keep it moistened with hydrogen peroxide until the mark has disappeared, or up to an hour. If the fibers have been burned the mark can't be removed, and on silks and woolens removal is always difficult. Tweeds or heavy woolens may look slightly improved if you gently rub the scorch mark with fine sandpaper or an emery board. You can avoid scorch marks by pressing on the wrong side when possible, and otherwise by using a pressing cloth.

When a garment's label directs that it should not be dry-cleaned, never use spot removers or dry-cleaning solvents containing chlorinated hydrocarbons (perchloroethylene or tetrachloroethylene). These solvents may damage fibers.

Washable Woolen, Unlined Linen, and Silk Fabrics

As soon as possible, run cold water through the stain on the garment, then immerse the entire garment or item in cold water and wash with a cold-water wash product. Apply the product directly to the stain. Rinse well and hang to dry. If, when dry, the stain remains, send the article to the dry cleaner.

Nonwashable Fabrics

Don't attempt to remove a stain yourself from a garment that you would normally have dry-cleaned. Take it to the cleaner and indicate specifically what caused the stain. Cleaners remove a majority of spots with a high-pressure water gun, but drying fabric without leaving water rings is in itself a painstaking job. Crepes, gabardines, moires, silks, satins, velvets, and some wools may be permanently marked by any sort of home treatment. If you are determined to experiment nonetheless, do so as follows:

Greasy stains. Back with an absorbent fabric or white blotting paper, sponge with Granny's Old-fashioned Stain Remover™, which is nontoxic, or with dry-cleaning solvent and repeat as necessary, drying between applications.

Nongreasy stains. Back with an absorbent material as above and sponge with cool water, penetrating the fibers completely. Apply liquid detergent directly and sponge it off with water. Remove all traces of detergent by sponging with denatured or rubbing alcohol, diluted with two parts water.

Combination stains. Treat as nongreasy, then as greasy, following the steps above.

Leather and Suede

Murphy Oil Soap, a natural soap containing vegetable oils and glycerin, will remove dirt from leather without harming its finish.

If a stain is greasy, you may be able to extract some of the oil by applying an absorbent powder, letting it dry, and repeating as needed.

Don't try to soften leather with lanolin, mink oil, or other animal fats. Animal fats are removed in leather processing because they become rancid and promote rot and decay, and reintroducing them may have the same effect. For heavy leathers, beeswax is appropriate and effective. It penetrates their natural state and protects against both moisture and drying out.

Fragile and Valuable Fabrics

When very fragile or valuable textiles need cleaning or repair, call your local art or textile museum and ask them to refer you to a textile conservator. Most conservators have their own workshops and will give your piece museum-quality attention at reasonable cost, regardless of its value or condition. Your neighborhood seamstress or dry cleaner may not be able to duplicate a conservator's resources and expertise and may inadvertently cause deterioration or damage.

If you have shopped in bridal boutiques, you know that a wedding dress may cost thousands of dollars; but a dress or veil that has been packed in a trunk for a generation or more can be restored with tender care to its original pristine state at a fraction of the cost, and will have the added value lent by tradition and sentiment.

Clothing Accessories

Handbags

∎

All leather objects need proper ventilation and 50 to 55 percent relative humidity to prevent either excessive drying or mildew growth. Don't store leather near steam pipes, which often run through closets.

To prevent scratching, marks, and dents, stuff handbags with tissue and keep in a dry place in flannel sacks.

Water damages leather. This will never be a problem if you fold a plastic shopping bag into a small square and tuck it into a corner of your handbag before you go out. Although bags should never be stored in plastic, it is far better occasionally to protect your bag with plastic for the afternoon than to let it get drenched in an unexpected downpour. If it does become wet, dry, condition, and polish the bag as soon as you are able.

Leather bags are difficult to clean, especially the new, very soft, buttery leathers, which are often woven in strips and absorb soil very easily. Wash leather with Murphy Oil Soap, and repolish from time to time.

19

There are many leather conditioners on the market; a favorite of handbag craftsmen is Saphir™. Use this on a regular basis to keep fine leather bags from drying and cracking.

Don't throw away a good leather bag that looks tired and bedraggled. Have it refurbished by a specialist. The expense is relatively small compared to the cost of a new bag, and a new bag is what it will look like. Worn edges, scuffs and nicks, holes in corners, and other stress points will disappear. Rusted or broken hardware and locks, cracked glaze, worn straps and handles, stained and torn lining, and wilted, limp interior structure will be replaced.

Leather can sometimes be dyed the same color if badly stained, or a lighter or darker color, although there is an ever-present risk of dyes cracking and peeling.

If you have an old alligator bag, have it remodeled. It can be taken apart and reassembled in any style for which there is enough material. This will cost hundreds of dollars, but it would cost thousands to replace it.

If a special evening bag has seen better days but has a wonderful frame and clasp, have a replacement bag custom-made. Many frames and clasps are invaluable.

Remember that a bag whose workmanship and material are the very best will last a lifetime. A bargain might not last out the season.

Shoes

Shoes should be kept on shoe trees to maintain shape and prevent creases, and if they are beaded, sequined, metallic, or made of light-colored fabric, they should be covered or kept in cloth bags.

Most shoe damage is caused by water. Stuff wet shoes with newspaper and let them dry slowly, away from heat. The paper will absorb moisture, so change it frequently if the shoes are thoroughly soaked. When dry, remove any salt stains by sponging with white vinegar. Polishing and conditioning on a regular basis will keep shoes supple and comfortable.

Shoe repairs can involve more than new soles and heels. A shoemaker can render nicks and tears virtually invisible. Very badly scuffed or stained shoes can be redressed, a process that strips, then restores the leather. Color can be changed, but the success of dyeing—always from light to dark—depends on the type and condition of the leather, and cannot be guaranteed.

Shoe-stretch products provide relief if shoes are just a bit tight, and conventional stretching will loosen them a bit more, but if your toes are still painfully squeezed, a cobbler can open the entire front of the shoe, add a strip of leather to match, and relast the shoe to the sole.

Specialists will also raise, lower, or replace heels, open or close toes, add or remove straps, or open heels to create sling-backs.

Fine shoes will last for many years, so if they are in excellent condition but no longer in vogue, give them a new look.

Gloves

Store fine gloves flat, separating each pair from the next by layers of acid-free tissue. When leather, suede, or kid gloves are stained or dirty, send them to a leather cleaner and they will be returned looking like new.

Jewelry

Jewelry is often damaged when carelessly stored. Individual pieces should be kept on soft, lint-free material or in tissue paper, and arranged so that each piece is separate. Don't store jewelry in cotton. Stones and prongs will catch on it, and cotton fibers will get beneath watch crystals and into the works.

Hard stones will scratch softer stones and all metals. Among precious stones, diamonds are the hardest, followed by sapphires and rubies, then emeralds. Bracelets or necklaces of stones should always be stored flat, so the stones don't touch each other.

After an evening out, many people casually drop their jewelry into a dish or onto a table, not realizing that the impact may cause stones to chip and settings to loosen. Watch crystals are easily loosened or broken. Sharp open clasps will scratch other pieces, and gold and silver are likely to dent.

To check periodically to be sure that prongs are firmly holding stones, shake them lightly. You may hear a faint click if the stones are loose. When concerned, or at least once a year, ask your jeweler to inspect and, if necessary, to tighten mountings. It is disconcerting, to say the least, to look down at your hand and see that you are wearing a setting without a stone—and it happens.

Dealers in precious stones and collectors use the simplest methods to clean all jewelry, including museum-quality pieces. They wash everything except wooden beads, beads strung on leather, and pearls, in soap and water. A soft brush gently eases out dirt from behind and between set stones. For stones and crystal, a little ammonia is added for a brilliant shine.

To keep pearls lustrous, wear them frequently, and if you have no occasion to wear them during the day, wear them to bed at night, as our grandmothers were told to do. Absolutely never allow pearls to come in contact with perfume, because its alcohol content will affect their color, their surface, and subsequently their value. Wipe pearls with a soft chamois cloth to remove dust, and check from time to time for signs of loosening knots or weakened string. Have them restrung as needed.

As beneficial as skin oils are to pearls, they are potentially harmful to turquoise, and may turn its natural blue to green. If this happens, use a very weak solution of hydrogen peroxide and water to restore the original color. Strengthen the mixture as necessary.

Excessive sunlight may dry turquoise and cause fading. The sun definitely fades kunzite and diminishes its value. So don't wear these stones to the beach.

The Gemological Institute of America grades diamonds and scientifically identifies pearls and other gemstones. Grading of diamonds includes description, measurement to a thousandth of a millimeter, weight to thousandths of a carat, proportion analysis, color gradation against a series of master stones, clarity gradation by binocular microscope, and plotting of identifying characteristics.

This analysis is called a GIA report. Before buying stones or pearls, ask to see it. In order to establish value of a piece of jewelry for insurance, request a GIA report from your jeweler. This service is available to members of the jewelry industry or directly to the public with a jeweler's letter of authorization. It's costly, a hundred dollars per carat for diamonds, but worth it if you are able to ascertain that your diamond is indeed worth trading for a villa on the Côte d'Azur or a few college educations.

Furs

Hang furs on extra-wide molded hangers that furriers supply or can tell you where to find. There are more than fifty types of fur on the market. Nearly all of them are heavy enough to stress the shoulder skins and seams dangerously if they are improperly hung.

Don't squeeze furs between other hanging garments or they will mat, and friction caused by removing them from the closet may cause shedding. Remove weighty objects from pockets, both when hanging and wearing furs, to prevent sagging seams.

Don't hang handbags, duffles, or briefcases with shoulder straps on the shoulders of fur coats as the friction may cause loss of fur hairs. If your fur is long-haired, take if off before sitting on velour seats or on similar snagging fabrics, such as those commonly used on seats in cars, planes, or trains. Friction from these surfaces may catch and break guard hairs, the long hairs that cover the underfur.

If your fur gets damp or wet, let it dry away from heat, then shake it out. Don't ever brush fur. If it is matted, always shake it. If you can't avoid your fur becoming completely drenched, let it dry slowly, then take it immediately to a furrier who does repairs, or the reverse (leather) side of the fur may pucker, resulting in a misshapen coat. The old adage that water never hurt the coat when the animal wore it is correct, but the animal is no longer wearing it.

Keep perfume away from fur. The alcohol can penetrate and dry out the leather. If fur is stained, gently blot the coat as much as possible and get it to a fur repair shop with haste. Give the shop as much detail as possible about the specific ingredients of the stain.

When carrying fur over your arm, turn it inside out as a safety precaution. If snagged or stained, the lining is easier to repair than the fur itself.

Excessive heat or humidity always damages fur. After a number of years, the natural oils on the leather side, which the living animal was able to replenish, inevitably begin to dry up. This drying process is slowed by cold storage, which provides an environment of approximately 40 degrees Fahrenheit and 50 percent relative humidity. Cold storage also prevents gradual discoloration and fading, and commercial cold storage includes moth protection as well.

If you cannot duplicate this environment at home, and in mid-moth season suddenly remember that you have forgotten to arrange cold storage, don't panic. An occasional year out of storage will not cause drastic damage. Moths, however, might. If you have space, place the fur in the freezer for forty-eight to seventy-two hours to kill any moth larvae present. Then drape a sheet over it and hang it in a cool, dry, mothproofed place or send it to storage.

Clean furs no more than every two years unless they are worn daily.

Cleaning and glazing are a single process. Furs are tumbled in a drum with cleaning fluids and an absorbent—usually sawdust or ground corncobs—for about two hours. When removed, the glazing process includes dematting and restoring a glossy shine. If the fur is very old, the tumbling may be overly stressful. Consider enjoying the coat for another few years as is.

Most fur repairs should be done by a professional. However, to sew up a minor split, get special thread, needle, and fur tape from a fur supply store. Open the lining and sew on the suede or leather side with an overhand stitch. Cut a piece of fur tape larger than the tear to fit over it, press the sticky side down, and smooth it out. Never iron furs on either side.

Patchwork Quilts

Patchwork quilting is an indigenous American art, and its products warm both body and spirit. Earliest examples date from the late eighteenth century and, although American quilting has not always enjoyed the popularity it does today, at no time since then has it ever died out.

Some quilts have been precisely and accurately planned, some haphazardly executed, some worked in the company of family or friends, and some in isolation. One made in Nebraska in the 1940s by Grace McCance Snyder, who learned quilting as a child to while away the hours she spent tending and herding cattle, is made of 87,000 pieces. Each of its squares, composed of two triangles, is three-eighths of an inch finished. But even the crudest and homeliest collage of patches represents hours of toil and care and elicits a warm response.

Ideally, quilts should lie flat, out of direct sunlight. If you have several extra, stack and rotate them on an unused bed, as the Amish do. Otherwise, roll them and store without bending the roll in the middle. Least preferred is to fold them, but if you do, keep the folds rounded

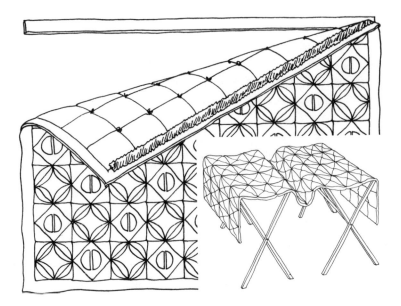

*Hang patchwork quilts by a Velcro strip that has been couched with a long
stitch through a firm border and runs the entire length of the top edge.
To dry a quilt, distribute the weight evenly over two folding clothes racks.*

■

by stuffing them with tissue, and refold them along new lines now and
then.

Gravity takes a toll on a quilt that is hung. Attach it with a long
stitch through firm seams to a weight-supporting fabric such as linen,
or suspend it from a Velcro™ strip that self-adheres or is stitched to the
length of the quilt's entire upper back edge and bears the quilt's full
weight. Ask a folk art dealer or a quilt restorer if there is a preferred
way to hang a particular piece, dictated by its construction and pattern
of stitching.

Many contemporary quilts can be machine washed and dried, but
unless you are so informed by a label, a maker, or a seller, hand-wash

it instead. First test colors for fastness; then clean the bathtub and remove every trace of scouring powder or detergent. Soak the quilt briefly in mild soap and tepid water. Rinse well, let it drain in the tub until the water no longer drips out when it is lifted, and dry on a sheet on the ground out of the sunlight, or distribute the weight evenly over two or more folding clothes racks. If hung over a line, the wet weight will break quilting stitches.

Don't wash a very old, fragile quilt under any circumstances, and never shake one. If necessary, gently hand-vacuum through fine soft netting. A strong power nozzle will tear out bits of fabric and thread.

For spots on white sections of a quilt, dab on a paste of cream of tartar and peroxy (all-fabric) bleach. After several hours, when it has dried to a powder, gently brush it off. For a badly stained quilt, see a textile conservator.

If a valued quilt needs restoration or repair, take it to a quiltmaker who dyes fabrics to match old colors.

And if it is too fragile to use comfortably at home any longer, give it to a museum or an organization with a quilt collection. They will ensure that it is mounted properly on a weight-supporting structure and displayed for brief periods or in special exhibitions, and the rest of the time it will provide a much-needed stable environment.

*R*ugs and Carpets

■

In the seventeenth and eighteenth centuries, very few rugs or carpets were found in this country. Those few wealthy Americans fortunate enough to own them used them not on the floor, but as coverings for beds, tables, cupboards, and other wooden furnishings.

Although the term "Oriental" has been loosely applied to carpets produced in Persia, Turkey, Greece, India, China, the Caucasus, North Africa, and Spain, seventeenth- and eighteenth-century "Orientals" came largely from Turkey, with an occasional few from India and Persia that probably reached the European Continent via the East India Company shipping routes.

Because "turkey carpets" were difficult to transport and too expensive for use on the floor, modest Colonial homes used floor coverings made of braided or hooked scraps of cloth or of painted canvas. But Turkish carpets predominated in the most aristocratic and impressive homes until the mid-1800s.

In the 1750s fashionable Americans began to import carpets from the Continent and England as well as from the Orient. Carpet industries burgeoned in the English towns of Axminster, Wilton, Moorfield, and Exeter, and upper-class Americans, ever anxious to emulate the styles set by their British cousins, began to use carpets more frequently on the floor than on furniture.

By the early nineteenth century American ships were trading directly with the Orient and a steady flow of goods began to appear, which, together with the hooked and braided carpets produced domestically, added warmth, color, and comfort to many American homes.

In 1791 the first American rug and carpet company opened in Philadelphia, followed by another in Worcester, Massachusetts, in 1804. Soon New York and New Jersey had their own small carpet industries, and in America floor coverings began to be regarded less as luxuries than as ordinary household effects.

Care and Cleaning

■

Older rugs and carpets are usually constructed of wool, silk, or cotton or some combination of them. At high temperature and humidity levels, mold grows easily on these natural fibers, and conversely, an excessively dry climate will cause them to become brittle. The healthiest environment for rugs and carpets is 70 degrees Fahrenheit and 50 percent relative humidity.

A carpet should be supported with underpadding to reduce wear, retard fiber breakdown, and prevent slipping. In rooms with heavy traffic flow, carpets should occasionally be turned to minimize wear in specific paths or patterns. Do this every six to twelve months with very valuable rugs.

If heavy furniture must be placed on a carpet, place legs on casters or rubber bases to avoid crushing the pile. Some casters have prongs that rest in the pile, raising furniture legs above it to prevent compression and resultant damage.

If the pile is crushed and can't be coaxed up by hand, place a damp cloth over the mark and apply a hot iron, using no pressure and barely touching the cloth. Then gently raise the pile by brushing. The same process of damp cloth and hot iron will flatten curled corners and edges.

Don't drag furniture on a carpet. Always lift it.

For storage, roll carpets, but not too tightly, as the carpets must be able to breathe. Don't stand them when rolled, and don't fold them.

Vacuum carpets weekly with the carpet attachment. Never shake or beat older, fragile rugs or hooked rugs. Don't vacuum hand-knotted fringed borders, which may be sucked into the vacuum, destroying part of the rug's foundation.

When our grandmothers were children, carpets were cleaned with damp tea leaves or wet Indian meal, tossed about and rubbed in with a broom. This was especially recommended for carpets made dingy by coal dust. Each spring, the clean carpets were rolled in tight linen bags whose crevices were stuffed with snuff, tobacco leaves, or bog-myrtle, as these scents would repel moths. Carpets left on the floor were protected by sprinkling them with pepper.

Today, in a more practical fashion, every two or three years carpets and rugs in good condition, except hooked rugs, should be washed by professionals who specialize in cleaning the type of rugs you own. If you decide to try rug shampoo products for at-home use, follow product directions meticulously, after testing for colorfastness. Do this by applying the cleaning solution to a small area, and after several minutes wipe the area with a clean white cloth. If the dye comes off on the cloth, the rug is not colorfast and should be sent to a professional rug cleaner.

Before shampooing or washing a rug, remove all loose dirt. If embedded dirt becomes wet it will form a muddy substance and may damage carpet fibers. To do this, turn the rug upside down or hang it on a clothesline. Gently shake it, and if it is a large rug, gently beat its back with a broom.

Remove spills and stains on carpets immediately. Blot up any excess liquid with absorbent towels or cloths. When no more liquid is absorbed by a dry cloth, sparingly pour soda water or seltzer over the stained area, and as its bubbles cause more of the spilled substance to surface, absorb it quickly with more dry towels or cloths.

Apply a special carpet spot cleaner such as Carbona Rug and Upholstery Cleaner™ according to label instructions, being careful not to soak the carpet and not to brush too roughly. Wipe off excess foam with a clean cloth. If no carpet-cleaning product is available, use detergent and water. Shake vigorously and apply the bubbly foam to the spot. Rinse well with white vinegar. This process works well on a myriad of stains, from red wine to urine. But speed is of the essence, for once set, most carpet stains are nearly impossible to remove completely.

For greasy stains, use a cleaning fluid, and sponge from the center of the stain toward the edge.

When a rug has been shampooed or washed, if furniture must be placed on it before it is thoroughly dry, place squares of folded waxed paper under furniture legs.

If you must walk on a damp rug, make yourself a path of waxed or brown paper, and don't stray from it until the rug is totally dry.

American Hooked Rugs

■

Hooked rugs have been produced in this country since Colonial times, originally as bed coverings and later for the floor.

Because their purpose was to provide warmth, they were usually lifted and stored in warmer months. This part-time usage doubled the

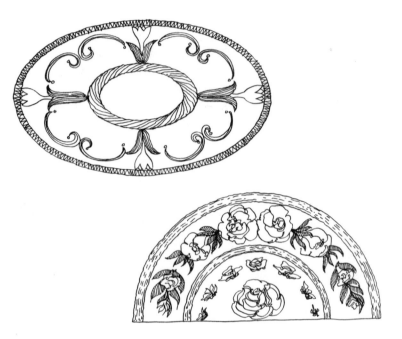

American hooked rugs were originally produced as bed coverings and later for the floor.

■

lifetime of many early American rugs, some of which remain in fine condition even today.

Always roll hooked rugs right side out, with the bottom of the rug on the inside of the roll. Otherwise the textile support, usually burlap, is likely to split.

If, after storage, a hooked rug is stiff or brittle, place a steam iron over a damp cloth, using very little pressure, and work the cloth and iron over the rug on both sides, section by section.

Brush the rug with foamy suds only, one small section at a time.

■

Don't commercially clean hooked rugs. Vacuum them gently, *not* with the power-nozzle attachment, and periodically wash them as follows. Mix ¼ cup of sudsy ammonia with two quarts of water. Brush the rug with the foamy suds only, a small section at a time. Rinse by

To preserve the textile support, always roll hooked rugs right side out.

■

33

brushing with clean water, then with white vinegar.

The rug-hooking industry is presently thriving in this country. If you have older hooked rugs in need of repair, consider restoration, and if you have a family heirloom that is beyond repair, have a reproduction of it hooked.

Although their origins were often in humble homes and their construction from fabric remnants or scraps of discarded clothing, many American hooked rugs are now at least as valuable as their Oriental counterparts.

Restoration

When valued rugs or carpets need repair or restoration, contact a textile conservator through your textile museum or a museum with a textile collection, or through the American Institute for Conservation of Historic and Artistic Works (see the "Sources and Services" chapter at the back of this book for the Institute's address and a list of museums by state). For restoration of hooked rugs, consult a local crafts museum or folk art museum, or a dealer in fine folk art.

*F*urniture and Wooden Objects

■

When a tree is cut, it dries out until its moisture level is in balance with the moisture level of its environment. At this point it is considered seasoned wood.

However, seasoned wood continues to respond to changes in environment by expansion and contraction. This is why it is often useless to restrain wood, to glue and clamp cracks, or to force a warp flat without addressing the cause of the wood's condition. Whatever caused the initial crack or warp may cause another crack or warp elsewhere in the piece.

Wood warps or splits due to its history of climate changes or to its original cut. If it was cut on a radius, it probably won't warp. If it has been parallel-sawed, it will tend to, in direct proportion to the distance of the cut from the center of the log. Often, cracks caused by dry heat disappear when sufficient humidity is restored, but are bound to recur if the piece is returned to the climate that first instigated them. In any case, only an experienced craftsman can advise whether repairs will protect the integrity of the structure.

The ideal environment for wood provides stability in temperature and relative humidity, protection from direct light, and protection from insects, fungus, and dry rot.

Wood's most suitable climate is an evenly maintained 68 to 70 degrees Fahrenheit, with relative humidity of 50 to 55 percent. Above 60 percent humidity, mold may begin to appear. However, sudden changes in temperature and humidity are even more perilous than a constant climate that is slightly damp, dry, cool, or warm.

Placement near any heating, cooling, humidifying, or dehumidifying source will subject wooden furniture to undue stress. Keep furniture and wooden objects at a safe distance from fireplaces, radiators, air conditioners, baseboard heaters, or cold outer walls. Remove excess humidity with a dehumidifier, and restore the loss of it with a humidifying machine.

Wood adapts very slowly, and the shock of turning on high air conditioning in midsummer heat, or of moving a piece of furniture from a heated home into an unheated van in near-freezing weather, can cause shrinking, cracking, checking, loose joints, and buckled veneer and marquetry.

Turning the heat suddenly from 50 to 68 degrees in your weekend house on Friday evening and back to 50 Sunday night is subjecting wooden furnishings to potential ruin, as is the intense heat in an uninsulated storage attic on a blistering summer day. Allow your wooden pieces to acclimatize slowly, and don't expose them to extremes of any sort.

Direct sunlight may dry and bleach wood, causing complete discoloration on the side of the piece facing the sun. If you have ever placed a mahogany table in a sunny bay window, you know that, well within a year, the side fronting the window can fade to a pale maple shade, while the finish becomes checked or alligatored as the sun's heat dries it out.

Materials are available to filter both direct and indirect light, but a simple preventive measure is to close blinds or shades whenever a room isn't in use.

Prolonged dampness invites dry rot. This, together with insects and fungus, requires treatment by the most skilled hands. Insect-ridden wood is tented with polyethylene, while DDVP or PDB is hung at the top of the tent. If a white film appears, the object is removed to dry for two or three days. Otherwise, treatment continues for a week, is discontinued for two weeks, and then the cycle is repeated to kill any newly hatched eggs. Fungus is killed with petroleum solvents (most commonly pentachlorophenol or copper naphthenate), and sections of dry rot, together with the areas surrounding them, must be completely removed.[*]

For any of these problems, consult a craftsman or conservator referred by the American Institute for Conservation of Historic and Artistic Works, by a museum with a furniture collection, or by a trusted source who knows from experience that the person recommended is knowledgeable and committed to protecting the integrity of each piece, not to merely masking its disfigured appearance. Referrals are not recommendations. Find out as much as you can about the conservation process and the conservation workshop to which you entrust your valued wooden furnishings. And keep exact documentation of repairs for reference during any subsequent restoration.

Surface Treatment of Wood

■

An ideal finish for wood incorporates stable color and adhesion properties, is reversible, resists abrasion, repels water, expands and

---

[*] Some materials used to treat or clean furniture have been linked to cancer. They include petroleum solvents and Lysol Spray. Do not inhale their fumes, and protect your hands with rubber gloves while using them. Dispose of materials and containers as you would hazardous waste.

contracts, and provides an aesthetically appealing and appropriate gloss.

Finishes commonly used are polyurethane, shellac, lacquer, boiled linseed oil, alone or mixed with turpentine and vinegar, and paste wax.

Carnauba, or microcrystalline-based paste wax, is the preferred treatment for all wood. It doesn't yellow or darken, won't break down chemically, is easily removed with 4-0 steel wool and turpentine, breathes and moves with wood, and produces a warm glow. It is only moderately successful as a water repellent.

Polyurethane, while completely moisture resistant, is generally irreversible, and doesn't permit wood to breathe. It must never be used on antiques.

Shellac, or shellac combined with oil to make French polish, dissolves readily with alcohol, but scratches easily and darkens with age. Nitrocellulose lacquers are also easily removed, but may break down chemically, turning white.

Boiled linseed oil, alone or in the traditional three-in-one combination with turpentine and vinegar, has fallen from favor, as has a favored recipe from our great-grandmothers' day: ¼ pint linseed oil, ¼ pint vinegar, 1 ounce spirits of salts, and ½ ounce muriatic antimony. Linseed oil darkens with age and is extremely difficult to remove.

All surface treatments are cosmetic and none replace lost moisture. Oils may penetrate wood, thus in fact harming its original finish, but they aren't absorbed by the wood's cells. *Wood cannot be fed.* Furthermore, oil attracts dust.

Wax, though preferred, builds up when overused and should be applied no more frequently than every two or three years. Once you are sure the surface is free of oily or sticky spots, apply paste wax in thin coats. A thin, evenly spread coating is easier to polish, won't smear, and gives a more lasting finish. Buff between layers until a clean cloth comes away clean. Be gentle with painted, inlaid, or damaged furniture.

Conservators recommend Renaissance Wax™, which was developed by a conservation scientist for the British Museum. It is a neutral blend of refined, microcrystalline waxes that are highly moisture resistant, prevent the milky discoloration known as bloom, and don't stain or discolor.

Renaissance Wax cleans and polishes wood and all other surfaces, including metal, marble, onyx, shell, stone, ivory, plastic, and even paper. Unless used sparingly, however, the wax may smear.

Cleaning Wood

■

Wood should be dusted regularly with a lint-free, hemmed duster. An unhemmed cloth will leave traces of lint, and threads may tear at splinters or catch and loosen molding, veneer, or marquetry.

Veneer or marquetry already loosened should be vacuumed through a screen or soft net. Vacuum lacquerware and painted furniture that has flaked or alligatored in the same way.

Don't use feather dusters. They can't be washed, and thus ultimately spread dirt instead of lifting it. And eventually the feathers break and scratch wood surfaces.

Under no circumstances use liquid or spray polish or wax on valued or valuable wood if they contain either silicone or acrylic resin. These ingredients seal wood, and wood that loses elasticity cannot breathe.

Dust-control sprays, whose main ingredient is mineral oil, moisten dust particles for easier pickup, but if applied to furniture rather than to a cloth they may streak or dissolve a wax finish. Many conservators and restorers consider them too heavy for regular use and recommend no sprays whatsoever. Murphy Oil Soap, a natural soap containing vegetable oils and glycerin, removes dirt from wood while preserving the wood's finish.

If a wood piece has been repeatedly spray-waxed, only a skilled technician should attempt to restore its original finish.

If your furniture is regularly cleaned by someone other than yourself, instruct that person meticulously about the methods and products you wish used. Otherwise you do your wooden furnishings a grave disservice.

Wood Repairs

In the course of living with our furniture we sometimes use and abuse it harshly. Some treatments for inadvertent accidents follow, but none are foolproof unless specifically recommended by a reliable technician. Remember always to rub wood in the direction of the grain.

Alcohol stains. Spilled drinks, perfumes, lotions, and medicines dissolve a number of finishes. Wipe up spills immediately, then rub the affected

Vacuum loose veneer or marquetry through a fine screen or soft net.

area with linseed, lemon, or another oil. In most cases you will need to mix a paste of powdered pumice or rottenstone and oil, apply it, and rub gently with the grain. This may be a job best left to a restorer, since home cure results aren't guaranteed.

Bloom. This milky discoloration is usually caused by excess moisture. Lemon oil, which contains petroleum distillate solvents, or paste wax, applied by cotton swab, may remove it, but chances are you need to consult a restorer for lasting results.

Burns. Treat a shallow surface burn as you would an alcohol stain. If the burn is deep, no topical care works, and you need to refinish.

Candle wax. Let the wax cool, or use an ice cube to harden it instantly. Then lift it with a rubber spatula. Wipe away remaining traces of wax with mild soap and lukewarm water and dry the spot thoroughly. To prevent wax from dripping, freeze candles for twenty-four hours before lighting them.

Checking and alligatoring. These fine crossed lines may result from excessive heat, or from an original finish having been applied to an incompatible base. Only refinishing will restore the surface, but careful application of paste wax can improve its appearance and curb flaking in the meantime.

Dents. If the depression is slight, wood can sometimes be made to swell and rise to the original surface level by applying a hot iron over several layers of moist cloth. Use as small a cloth as possible to cover the dent since the finish may be marred by the wet heat. If it is, lightly apply camphor oil, peppermint oil, or turpentine with a cotton swab, and follow with clear water, or use powdered pumice or rottenstone mixed to a paste with lemon oil. If none of these is on hand, rub in the proverbial cigar ash, with the grain, wipe with linseed oil, and rewax.

Slight dents in wood can be made to swell and rise to the original surface by carefully and briefly applying a hot iron over several layers of moist cloth.

■

Food and grease stains. Lightly dampen a soft cloth with mild soap or Murphy Oil Soap and lukewarm water and wipe away food and grease. Dry the treated area and rewax if necessary, rubbing and buffing in the direction of the grain.

Heat marks. Stroke the spot lightly with a cloth dipped in camphorated oil and wipe immediately with a clean cloth. If necessary, make a paste of rottenstone and oil and use a soft clean cloth to rub it into the wood.

Mildew. Mildew occurs in damp, airless locations. Brush off the spores outdoors to avoid scattering them in the house. Wash the piece with mild soap and dry it in the sun. If traces of mildew remain, sponge them lightly with denatured or rubbing alcohol and rewash. As a last resort, mist the affected area with Lysol Spray, a solution of orthophenylphenol in ethanol. (Use only the spray; Liquid Lysol is formulated differently.) Then wipe off traces of mist.

Nicks and scratches. An experienced restorer should deal with deep scratches or gouges, but you can often camouflage superficial nicks or scratches on wood with one of a number of treatments: a Zenith Tibet Almond Stick™; colored crayons from a child's crayon set; wax sticks that are made in a number of wood tones; nutmeats; the burnt end of a match; iodine, or iodine mixed with denatured alcohol or linseed oil to soften the color. Paste shoe polish can be applied with a cotton swab; if it is too dark, partially remove the polish with mineral spirits until it blends in. Paste polish will buff to a luster, so don't use it if the finish on the piece is very dull.

Water spots. A properly waxed finish guards against most water spots if they are quickly wiped up with an absorbent cloth and the surface is dried. If a spill leaves a foggy mark, rub it lightly and briefly with a cotton swab dampened with Orvis WA Paste or with denatured or rubbing alcohol. Then wipe it clean and dry, and carefully reapply a thin coating of paste wax. Always wipe with the grain.

White rings. White rings left by hot or cold containers can be effaced completely if caught right away, while the blemish is in the polish but has not yet affected the finish. Vigorously rub in a thin paste of wood ashes and salad oil or lemon oil, butter, margarine, or mayonnaise. If the mark is still evident, sprinkle a folded cloth with a few drops of ammonia and rub gently and quickly with a circular motion. For persistent stains, try a paste of oil and rottenstone and rub well with the grain, or a paste of oil and 4F Pumice Powder,™ then rewax.

When wooden furnishings need restoration, locate a conservator or restorer of the highest caliber. An unskilled job may strip away the surface of the wood, damage its fibers, or change hardwood colors. An experienced technician will protect the integrity of the piece, working with reversible materials to facilitate subsequent restoration when and if it is necessary. If you do it yourself, keep in mind that driving nails or drilling holes splits the grain and leads to cracks, and loosens joined parts, although evidence of damage may appear at some distance from the nail or drilled hole. The American Institute for Conservators of Historic Works, a museum with a furniture collection, or a knowledgeable collector can refer you to a local conservator or restorer (see "Sources and Services," at the back of the book, for addresses). Confirm a reference with a recommendation whenever possible.

Bamboo, Wicker, and Baskets

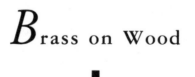

To clean bamboo, wicker, and woven baskets, vacuum with the dusting attachment brush to reach cracks and crevices and extract dirt trapped in the weave. If dirt remains, spray cool water through the weave or strips as forcefully as necessary to remove it. Efface spots with mild soap and water. Use a blow-dryer on high air setting to hasten drying.

Brass on Wood

To clean bamboo, wicker, and woven baskets, vacuum with the dusting attachment brush to reach cracks and crevices and extract dirt trapped in the weave. If dirt remains, spray cool water through the weave or strips as forcefully as necessary to remove it. Efface spots with mild soap and water. Use a blow-dryer on high air setting to hasten drying.

Whether or not to polish brass fittings on wood is a matter of aesthetic choice. Most museum staffs now prefer that brasses not gleam brightly, but be allowed to tone down to a soft patina. They advise polishing as occasionally as you should the wood, every two or three years, using the same paste wax.

This makes life infinitely easier for the polisher; polishing brass is one of the most arduous and energy-demanding household tasks.

If brasses are in good condition and you want to shine them, remove them from furniture, as the energetic buffing required to heighten the shine will mar the surrounding wood. Many old brasses are handmade and too fragile to be removed. In this case try to slip a piece of aluminum foil between brass and wood to protect the wood. Polish vigorously with brass polish, and then remove all polish residue, which is corrosive. If there is a buildup of residue, remove it with equal parts of ammonia and water on a natural bristle toothbrush, rinsing well with clean water to neutralize the ammonia afterward.

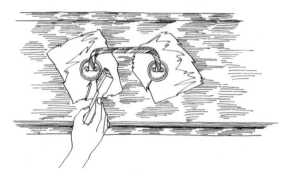

When old, handmade brasses are too fragile to remove for polishing, slip aluminum foil behind the brass to protect surrounding wood from polish and from buffing strokes.

*M*arble

Cleaning methods have become relatively simple since the days when grease was removed from marble by coating it with a mixture of a gill each of ox-gall, potter's clay, soapsuds, and spirits of turpentine. The mixture was left on for two days, then removed by rubbing vigorously.

Clean and polish marble tabletops or lamp bases with Renaissance Wax. Use a mild detergent, but only one time, on light stains. Repeated usage will yellow and streak the stone. Consult a stone or marble specialist for dark stains. Guard against them by applications of Renaissance or other paste wax, or with commercial marble sealers.

To remove stains from marble, make a solution of hydrogen peroxide with several drops of ammonia. Apply it and leave it on for several hours. Remove it with a clean cloth and wipe away traces of the solution with cold water.

Pianos

■

Pianos are magnets for moths and mice, which nest inside, chewing and eating felts and hammers. Ask your tuner to mothproof the interior or to recommend someone who will, and place mouse repellent behind the piano's base.

An electric heat bar designed for pianos helps keep the piano's interior dry if it is in a damp location.

To prevent dust from wedging and collecting between keys, dust them from back to front with repeated short, swift strokes. If dust has already gathered between keys, vacuum them with a strong power nozzle.

If little fingers or careless guests get ivory keys dirty, clean with a damp cloth. Lift key slightly with your finger to see that no water is left between the keys.

Keep the keyboard cover raised. Closing it traps moisture and may cause the keys to swell or warp.

Upholstery

■

In mid-nineteenth-century households, curtains, ottomans, and sofas covered with worsted were cleaned by rubbing them all over with wheat bran and flannel cloths. Today, we advise that you vacuum furniture upholstery weekly. Remove cushions and use the crevice attachment to reach deeply along the sides and back of the springs. If your cushions are filled with down, vacuum them with the dusting attachment brush, since the power nozzle may draw feathers through the fabric. Use the same attachment along seams or ribbing, and in and around tufts and depressed buttons.

In our grandmothers' day, washable antimacassars were placed on the backs and arms of upholstered furniture to prevent soiling; most fabrics today are protected with stain-resistant chemicals, and vacuuming on a regular basis is sufficient to keep them in good, clean condition.

Protection and Handling

■

Protect frequently used wood surfaces by covering them with beveled-edged glass tops cut to size. Place felt disks beneath the glass at its corners to lift it and allow air flow. If spilled liquid seeps beneath the glass, lift it and dry both glass and wood to avoid stains that might appear from condensation.

To prevent scratches on bare wood surfaces, pad lamp bases and place cork or felt disks, or felt or chamois mats, under all vases, plants, or other objects. Certain porcelain objects are especially prone to scratch or gouge wood surfaces, because their bases are unglazed, and extremely rough and sharp.

Plants should be placed so their leaves don't touch the wood. Flowers that drip nectar onto wood are likely to produce irreversible acid stain.

Don't cover wood with plastic cloths or mats. The ingredients in many plastics will migrate to wood, especially under conditions of high heat and relative humidity, or when plastic is weighted down by a heavy object such as a filled vase. The resultant damage will most likely require refinishing.

Don't overload drawers. If they have two handles, use both of them to open and close, or you risk transverse jamming and splits in the seams where the drawer front joins sides and bottom. If drawers stick, don't force them. Rub soap, candle wax, paste wax, or beeswax along runners. If they continue to stick, they may need light sanding.

Don't push or drag furniture. Lift pieces by a solid part of the framework, such as a chair by its seat and not by its arms, and never lift a piece by a projecting or ornamental part.

To lift a wooden object such as a chest or box, support it from beneath. Don't lift by handles or knobs, which may be decorative and incapable of supporting the object's full weight. Remove drawers before lifting a desk or bureau.

Children have been instructed for years, and rightly so, not to tilt back in their chairs. Tilting back a chair while you are seated dangerously weakens its frame and all its joints and struts, and resultant stress may cause the chair's seat or legs to crack or its joints to separate. Using your feet or legs to push a chair backward while you are sitting in it has the same result. Instead, lift your body weight from the chair as though in order to stand, move the chair backward, and sit again.

If the cane seats of chairs begin to sag, wash them in very hot water and dry them in the sun.

Paintings

We are accustomed to thinking of paintings on canvas as flat surfaces, but a painting on canvas is a complex, three-dimensional structure of several strata. Its construction includes the stretcher that bears the canvas; the woven fabric of the canvas support; the priming coat; the paint film or films, including layers of overpainting or inpainting; and, usually, a final protective coat of varnish.

The stretcher is a wood frame with parallel sides. Corners must be square or the canvas is pulled out of shape. Creases or ripples originate at acute-angled corners and fan diagonally across the canvas. At obtuse angles, the tension may cause splits or fractures in the canvas or paint film.

The canvas, or fabric support, is the painting's base. It must be evenly and firmly tacked to the stretcher edge to prevent puckering or sagging. Like all textiles, canvas dries and weakens as it ages, and it requires periodic monitoring.

The priming is the coat that seals the threads of the woven fabric and the interspaces between them. It assures that the paint rests on the canvas surface and isn't absorbed into the weave.

A painting on canvas is composed of several layers: the stretcher, the canvas support, the priming coat, the paint layer, and usually a protective coat of varnish.

■

The paint film is pigment in a medium. The pigment, or color, is composed of particles of solid matter. These are borne in a fluid substance, the medium, which carries the pigment. The medium must adhere well, dry evenly and fairly quickly, and shouldn't interfere with or affect the color as it dries. On canvas, traditional media are acrylic or oil. A lean paint film has less medium than pigment, not the other way around. It's referred to as lean because as the small amount of medium dries out, the paint particles rest lightly on the canvas. A rich paint film's proportions are reversed.

The protective coat, or varnish, is the paint film's guard against airborne dirt, which rests on the varnish instead of on the paint. Many folk art paintings are unvarnished, and there is a trend toward a matte finish on twentieth-century paintings, but it is possible to control a varnish's gloss by using a dull-finish film that doesn't appreciably change a painting's appearance. Unvarnished paintings are difficult to clean, because you are working directly on the paint film, and in removing dirt you are likely to remove paint as well. Varnish darkens and discolors or yellows with age, may fog or scratch, and over a period of years may need cleaning and replacing so it must necessarily be reversible, and should also resist moisture as efficiently as possible.

Finally, the adhesion of layers is known as the bond. This must be strong enough so that the strata don't separate when one layer moves in response to changes in temperature or humidity.

*E*nvironment

■

Paintings on canvas are always in motion; they respond to environmental fluctuations as wood does, by expanding and contracting. To minimize possible resultant damage, don't hang them on cold, outer stone walls or on inner walls warmed by the furnace flue; over thermostats, radiators, or air conditioners; or in the path of hot or cool air vents. Shield venting units to deflect the flow of airborne dirt and soot. If a painting hangs over a fireplace, plan to have it checked at least every two years by a restorer.

Heat may cause flaking of paint, and excessive heat will blister and ultimately powder the fabric support. Rapid or dramatic fluctuation in environmental conditions may cause bulging, peeling, or warping.

Light is also destructive to paintings. Shade windows and lamps, or photochemical reactions may immeasurably alter the way a painting looks.

Hanging Paintings

■

To allow air circulation behind frames, place small cork pads on the backs of frames at the lower corners to keep the lower frame edge from resting on the wall.

Wrap adhesive tape around the middle of the hanging wire or cord where the wall hook supports it, or use two wall hooks approximately two inches apart, so the painting won't tilt to a crooked position on the wall.

More paintings are damaged by falling off the wall than in any other way. The frame and the hardware that supports it must be strong enough to bear the painting's full weight.

With time plaster moves, wall hooks loosen, stretcher nails and keys

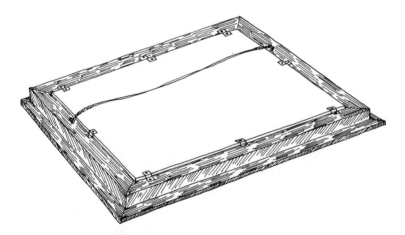

Protect the canvas back with a piece of process board or other strong mat board attached to the back of the frame.

■

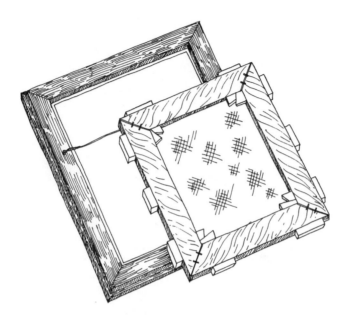

*To expose the painting's entire surface within the frame,
enlarge the stretcher with added strips; these strips rest against the
rabbet, and the entire paint surface can be seen.*

■

fall out, wire rusts, and cord slackens. Check these, and screw eyes, regularly, because vibrations from appliances, from high decibel levels, and even from footsteps can loosen hardware. Remember too that excess picture wire may press against the back of the canvas and bulge it out. Firm and secure hanging is inexpensive and reliable insurance against the most common of disasters, the crash of a painting onto the floor.

You would be horrified if this happened to the madonna in its heavy frame that your ancestor the ambassador brought back from Rome and that you have cherished for years.

Always protect the back of canvas with a piece of process board or other strong mat board cut to size, which also keeps out dirt.

To hang a painting so that its entire surface can be seen, enlarge the stretcher with strips added to its four sides. The added strips then rest against the rabbet, or inner edge of the frame, and the entire painting is fully exposed.

*L*oosened Stretchers

■

A changing environment may cause a loosened stretcher and a slack canvas. Observe the condition for six or eight weeks. If the sagging

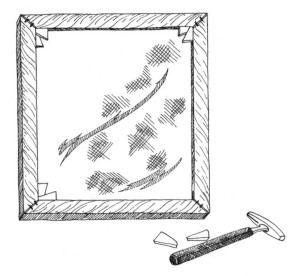

Loose stretcher keys should be wedged in tightly to spread the corner joints and tighten the canvas.

■

doesn't reverse, the stretcher must be tightened, or ripples in the paint film may develop into cracks and breaks.

Sometimes the stretcher and canvas can be tightened by keying the stretcher out. You can do this if there are two triangular pieces of wood, or keys, in each frame corner. If the painting is large and heavy, they may be found inserted at the corners of the cross-supports as well.

These keys must be wedged in tightly with a tack hammer to spread the corner joints, enlarging the stretcher and thereby tightening the canvas.

If the stretcher is nailed at the corners instead of keyed, it is known as a strainer. Strainers can't be enlarged, and a restorer must be asked to carefully restretch and retack the canvas along the strainer edge.

Storage

When a painting is removed from the wall, both of its sides are exposed and vulnerable. For storage, lean one or more paintings against the wall of an empty room or an empty closet. If a closet is in use, be sure the painting is positioned so that shelved or hanging articles will not fall on the painting and damage it.

To store more than one canvas, separate them with acid-free process board or masonite to prevent damage to one from the frame or hardware of the other.

Prevent the bottoms of frames from sliding by padding them with towels or pillows.

If paintings are stored in rooms that are being decorated, and there is even the very slightest danger of splatter, cover them with sheets of polyethylene. Don't use painter's cloths, which are notoriously dusty and dirty.

Moving

■

Moving paintings on canvas poses a special problem. They are extraordinarily vulnerable to abrasion, fracture, and perforation.

You would be wise to read this before transporting the portraits of your Dutch forebears that always hung in your mother's dining room.

To move a painting in its frame, wrap it with glassine or bubble wrap, and tie it between two pieces of strong process board cut at least two inches larger than the outer edge of the frame. If the frame is ornate, protect its corners with extra bubble wrap.

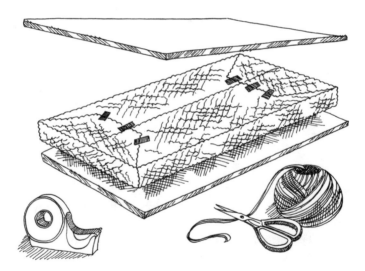

For transport, paintings should be wrapped with bubble wrap and tied between two process boards.

■

Professional movers know precisely how to wrap paintings for transit and will perform this service for you whether or not they are doing the actual moving.

There are also professional packers, who will use a "mirror box" when appropriate, with bubble wrap inside and out, and who will arrange for safe, insured shipping if you so desire.

Unframed paintings may be removed from the stretcher and rolled for packing by a restorer or professional framer referred by the Professional Picture Framer Association.

Because moving paintings on canvas immeasurably increases the risk of injuring them, always insure them in transit, either by a rider on your homeowner's or fine arts policy, or by a special policy available from the moving company.

Routine Cleaning

■

Paintings on canvas should be dusted frequently with a silk cloth, a very soft brush such as a sable or camel's hair brush, or a photographer's blower brush, through which air is forced by a rubber bulb. Don't use ordinary dusting cloths, because cracks in paint snag easily, and some are present in virtually every paint film surface. By using a cloth on Uncle Charlie's portrait, you may inadvertently remove his nose or eyes with one swipe. Be sure always to remove all traces of dust, because it frequently contains airborne mold spores.

The old practice of cleaning paintings with halved raw onion or potato removes some surface dirt, but these materials are too rough on delicate brushstrokes, and they leave a film on paint, just as they do on the kitchen counter.

Clean the backs of paintings also, dusting gently and checking to be

*A photographer's blower brush is an effective tool for removing
surface dirt and dust from paintings.*

■

sure no plaster or other debris is lodged in the crevice between the
stretcher and the canvas. A slipped stretcher key or even a certain
amount of dirt that has accumulated there will cause bulging in the
front of the canvas along the stretcher edge. Gently tap it out,
changing the painting's position as necessary.

Cleaning by a Conservator

■

Every two or three years a conservator should check paintings on canvas
and remove surface dirt and grime. Cleaning won't lengthen a

painting's life, but it may change its colors and appearance astoundingly, especially in cities and urban areas, where dirt is often greasy black soot. Many people aesthetically prefer the patina of age, but if tonal values are lost because they are obscured by dirt, it may be time for a serious professional cleaning.

The cleaning process is complex and its steps are governed by a painting's condition, environmental history, bond, medium, pigment, or the type of varnish orginally used.

If you have not extended the stretcher, the strip of painting under the frame often testifies to original colors, but colors clean differently, and some may seem to recede while others leap out from the surface. White is generally stable, black tends to bleed, and the entire spectrum varies.

Ask your conservator for a detailed explanation of what color changes you may expect and how they might be minimized.

*R*estoration

■

When restoring a painting, do only what is absolutely necessary to hold it together and in place.

Ask your local art museum or the American Institute for Conservation of Historic and Artistic Works (see "Sources and Services" for addresses) to refer you to a conservator, who must understand chemistry and physics, and should be an art historian, a skilled diagnostician, and a well-trained practitioner—a veritable Renaissance person.

Also, a conservator must submerge his or her personality and attempt to observe a painting through the eyes of its painter. This may sound presumptuous, but it would be far more presumptuous to impose the conservator/restorer's own artistic thinking on someone else's inspired visual concept.

The traditional financial plight of the artist, together with the painter's penchant for ever more innovative ideas, has often led to the use of inexpensive, impermanent, and undesirable materials. Thus, some deterioration may be unavoidable despite all precautions.

Willem de Kooning has used salad oil and water in his paint, Jackson Pollock has used ordinary house paint, and Frank Stella has used metallic enamel. Other contemporary painters are using materials that range from Day-Glo™ to last night's dinner, generating a need for fresh thinking and creative conservation procedures if their original work is to survive at all.

Whether a painting is twenty or two hundred years old, all diagnostic methods need to be considered and correctly interpreted to reach a satisfactory prognosis and proposal for treatment. Ultraviolet examination can record composition of strata, infrared can record facets of substrata, and X ray can record density, concealed images, and otherwise imperceptible damage.

The binocular microscope exposes a canvas layer in such detail that it reveals even different-sized color particles, or pigment, in the medium, and chemical and microchemical analysis can identify and date materials used originally or in subsequent restoration.

Badly weakened canvas may be lined with a new fabric support behind the original. If a painting has already been lined, you will see two canvases at the tacking edge. However, lining requires uniform pressure on the entire paint surface, which may flatten the texture to a point where a good deal of the painter's visual concept is lost as all trace of the brushstrokes vanishes.

As a final drastic measure, if the fabric support is rotting or destroyed, the painting can sometimes be meticulously transferred to a new support.

A torn painting can be mended or even patched, as long as the slightly raised outline of the patch doesn't detract from the congruity of the design. Most tears can be repaired, but if they are left untreated for any length of time they will curl, distorting surrounding sections of the painting and resulting in cracked, flaked paint. If a painting is torn and you are unable to reach a conservator immediately, use masking tape on the back of the canvas to keep the fabric support flat and the frayed threads from unraveling.

As a painting expands and contracts, absorbing and releasing moisture, its strata may dry out and become brittle to a point of no further flexibility. Cracks then erupt in the priming, which may soon rise to the surface. If untended, these cracks progress to cleavage, and if you are able to see threads of the canvas support, the situation has become disastrous.

Under normal conditions, a painting expands and contracts, but if expansion causes sagging of the canvas, a conservator should be called.

If expansion is enough to cause sagging of the canvas, other cracks may appear where the canvas edge is restrained by the stretcher strip.

Still other cracks may originate in the paint layer. These seldom penetrate lower layers, but if they detract from the design or endanger substrata, they may be filled with gesso or inpainted. Gessoing, inpainting, and overpainting must be kept to a bare minimum but are sometimes expedient means to retard deterioration at an early stage, and they can often be accomplished without greatly modifying the painter's integral concept.

Lesser problems restorers may confront are bulges from picture wire or from objects protruding behind the canvas. These protrusions are usually dampened and weighted to dry.

Tangled or protruding picture wire may cause bulging of the canvas paint surface.

■

A common problem needing a conservator's attention is bloom, the milk-white film that appears on varnish. This is usually removed by an application of mild paste wax, or Renaissance Wax, and cotton swabs. The wax is gently wiped off until the cloth comes away clean. A waxed finish won't bloom, but wax alters a painting's appearance and is not aesthetically appropriate most of the time.

Always ask a conservator for a written proposal and estimate before a restoration is begun, and insist on photographs documenting work before treatment, when the painting is in a stripped-down state, and after completion. These are critical for appraisal, insurance, or resale of a painting, and facilitate subsequent restoration when and if it later becomes necessary.

Works of Art on Paper

■

Paper was discovered nearly two thousand years ago, allegedly by a Chinese eunuch named T'sai Lun, who hammered scraps of precious woven fabric, which was used at the time for writing, until he reduced the entire mass to fibers. He mixed the fibers with water and poured the mixture onto a screen. The water drained away and the matted fibers dried, becoming the first known sheets of paper.

Soon other papermakers were working with bamboo, hemp, and mulberry bark, from which Japanese rice paper is still made.

By the thirteenth century, papermaking had spread to Italy, France, Germany, and Spain, where the linen and cotton rags used acted as blotters, bleeding and feathering the ink from quill pens. European craftsmen devised a warm gelatin dip to give their paper a harder, more resilient surface. This process is known as sizing.

The fifteenth-century invention by Johann Gutenberg of movable type created widespread demand for paper; the seventeenth-century invention of the Hollander machine, with its high-speed metal blades, produced smooth pulp with speed and efficiency. The paper it yielded was weaker, with shorter fibers, but 50 to 100 percent more of it was realized from each batch of rags.

Also in the seventeenth century, alum was introduced as a sizing agent, with disastrous long-term results, as it greatly increased acidity and reduced longevity in generations of paper to follow.

In this country, William Rittenhouse of Germantown, Pennsylvania, is known to have made paper as early as 1690. In 1867 the first groundwood pulp mill in the United States opened in Stockbridge, Massachusetts, and American newsprint was born. The wood pulp and alum present in varying degrees in paper produced between 1850 and 1950 proved a perilous combination, because alum compounds break down into acids that devour the bond holding the wood pulp fibers together. Paper so produced and left untreated eventually disintegrates.

For purposes of longevity, paper should be made from acid-free, alum-free pulp produced from purest fibers of cotton and high-alpha cellulose. Some papers are buffered with alkali for increased protection against present and future acidic contaminants, intrinsic or extrinsic.

Archival papers are also lignin-free. Lignin is an ingredient of wood that binds cellulose, and a papermaker's yield per tree is increased from 35 to 95 percent by using it, but it will greatly hasten the paper's demise by emitting a variety of acids and peroxides. Because lignin is photosensitive, it dries and makes paper that is exposed to light brittle as well.

Buffered archival paper can be expected to last well in excess of three hundred years.

Paper in its many forms is commonly found in every home, and by ordinary daily exposure to it, many of us have come to believe it is indestructible. But if you have saved any newspaper clippings, paperback books, or paper souvenirs for twenty years, you know that even in that brief period they may become yellowed and begin to crumble.

Environment

■

Paper is ultrasensitive to light and heat. Works of art on paper should be illuminated by no more than five foot-candles, or approximately 150 watts at a distance of three to four feet. This can be measured by a photographer's light meter calibrated in foot-candles.

Ultraviolet (UV) filtering materials reduce potential damage by removing light's most dangerous component, but other rays are still damaging. Infrared converts to heat and causes buckling or flaking. Virtually all light fades works of art on paper. The bluer the light, the more damage it causes. Shades of yellow to red are so minimally harmful as to be considered nearly innocuous, but these light colors do little to enhance the decor of a room in which artworks are displayed.

Temperature for paper should be 68 to 70 degrees Fahrenheit. High heat weakens paper and makes it brittle, and combined with high humidity, invites mold. Humidity should be kept at 40 to 50 percent. Above 65 percent, mold and fungus flourish, and rapid oxidation takes place.

Temperature fluctuation of as little as 18 degrees Fahrenheit may drastically increase the rate of fading of fugitive colors.

Some colors that are most fugitive and easily damaged by poor environment are vegetable-based dyes such as safflower and turmeric in Japanese prints; drawings in iron gall ink, used prior to the late 1800s, which fades from purple-black to dingy brown; late nineteenth-century lithographs and aquatints, such as Currier & Ives and English hunting prints; and any works of art on paper with a high groundwood content.

Many types of paper are deteriorating at the same accelerating rate with which pollution escalates. Paper's worst enemy is acidity, including sulfur dioxide, a major component of smog. This causes discoloration, embrittlement, and ultimate disintegration. Installation of air conditioning, and front and back acid-free mats sealed to prevent exposure to air, reduce the effects of sulfur dioxide and other powerful atmospheric contaminants.

Whether acid is a product of the chemical process used in manufacturing, of pollution, or of contact with acidic materials, paper can now be chemically treated to provide greater protection against all forms of acid reaction. Paper can't be considered durable and permanent if its pH factor is below 6. To prolong its life-span, it is chemically buffered to as high a factor as 10.5 on the scale of 1 to 14.

Finally, environmental conditions can combine to attract silverfish, termites, cockroaches, woodworms, mice, and other pests to paper. When these are found, a conservator must recommend specific insecticide remediation, which is often achieved by exposing infected paper to DDVP or PDB.

Matting

■

When pictures are shown in frames, a mat permits breathing space between the work of art on paper and the glass that covers it, allowing the paper to move. Never mount paper directly against the glass. Glass not only condenses moisture, encouraging growth of mold when there is no air circulation behind it, but also is prone to electrostatic charge. As glass catches and retains the surface of the paper, static may transfer the design to the glass. Pastels and charcoals are extremely vulnerable to this adhesion.

If for practical or aesthetic reasons you prefer not to mat a picture, use separating strips on the paper under the rabbet or inner rim of the frame. These serve the same purpose as a mat by permitting air flow,

*If a picture is framed without a mat, separating strips
under the frame rim permit air flow and prevent both mold growth
and static transfer of design from paper to glass.*

■

to prevent both mold growth and static transfer of design from paper
to glass.

Mats should be acid-free, buffered museum board or all-rag mat
board. Wood pulp mat board contains groundwood, which disintegrates and in the process leaves brown stains on the paper it rests
against.

A picture should be hinged to the back of its mat so it hangs freely
and moves easily. Tab or pendant hinges should be made of Japan
tissue or acid-free pressure-sensitive tape such as Filmoplast 90™, as
thin as possible to support safely the weight of the paper they hold, and
if Japan tissue is used it should attach paper to mat with water-soluble
rice or wheat-starch paste.

Never use Scotch Tape™, other pressure-sensitive tape, or rubber cement on works of art on paper. These adhesives cause irreversible brown stains.

Framing

■

Frames should be well sealed on both sides. The back of the mat should be covered with acid-free board and the gap between board and frame sealed with gummed brown wrapping tape, which is permeable and responds to fluctuations in environment.

Many old frames were backed with cedar shingles, corrugated cardboard, or wood. These backings transfer patterns of knots, ripples, or grain to the face of the paper, and should be removed and replaced with acid-free backings as soon as possible.

Don't frame paper between two pieces of glass. This doubles the risk of mold growth. If it is necessary to see both sides of the paper, frame it between sheets of acrylic plastic (Plexiglas™, Lucite™, Permacryl™). This material is also suitable for very heavy or large frames, because it is lightweight and shatterproof.

However, acrylic plastic is even more prone to electrostatic charge than glass, and shouldn't be used for charcoals or pastels or it will lift their designs from the paper. So will traditional frosted, nonglare glass. A nonglare glazing suitable for works of art on paper is Denglas™.

Err on the side of caution and select extra-heavy hardware for frames. Use two separate wall hooks to hang large or heavy frames safely and securely. Gummed, self-adhesive hooks aren't safe for any long-term hanging or for frames of any appreciable weight.

Wrap adhesive tape around the middle of the picture wire where it rests on the wall hook to prevent frames from tilting to a crooked position on the wall, or use two hooks to keep a frame firmly and squarely placed.

Every ten years, a framer or restorer should open frames, inspect works of art on paper, and clean the inside surface of the glass before reframing.

Too much pressure from a mat or frame may cause buckling of paper, as may old glue or tape on the back of it. If buckling of framed paper occurs for any reason, a conservator or paper restorer can advise how to reverse it.

Cleaning

In routine home cleaning, dust frames and glass frequently. Dust contains airborne mold spores, which if left to migrate may work themselves under the edge of the glass and onto the paper.

Don't attempt to clean the outside surface of the glass by spraying it. Moisture and drops of cleaning spray are almost certain to seep beneath the edge of the glass at the rabbet or inner rim of the frame. Spray a cloth sparingly and wipe the glass clean.

Gilt frames should be dusted gently with a soft cloth. This is a far less arduous task than the treatments recommended in the mid-nineteenth century, when gilt was preserved with a coat of copal varnish obtained from a carriagemaker or a cabinetmaker, or could be brightened with enough sulfur to give a golden tinge to 1½ pints of water, boiled with four or five bruised onions. When this was strained, chilled, and washed over the gilding, the frame was supposed to look like new.

Storage

■

Store works of art on paper flat, in acid-free, lignin-free boxes or cases or in solander boxes. Interleave paper with acid-free board or tissue. For best results, protect paper in storage with acid-free mats as well.

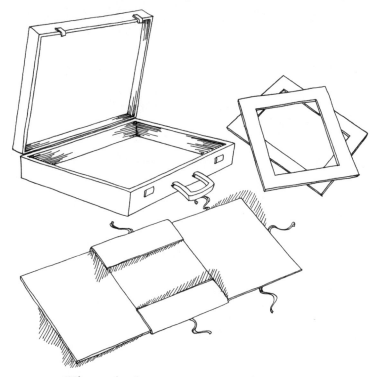

When works of art on paper are stored in solander boxes or other cases, interleave them with acid-free board or tissue and protect them with acid-free mats.

■

Works of art on paper are sometimes protected from damage in storage by encapsulation between two sheets of clear, polyester film, closed at the edges by 3M No. 415™ double-sided tape. To do this, keep a space of one inch between the tape and the edge of the paper enclosed. Some papers should be acid-neutralized before they are sealed. Don't encapsulate paper unless it is in very good condition, and unless the process used is easily reversed.

Mold spots, or foxing, will appear on paper stored in humidity of over 65 percent. Mold feeds on both fiber and sizing, greatly weakening paper, and it grows particularly easily on pastels.

You can prevent mold in storage areas with small dishes or sachets of thymol. If you are storing a number of works of art on paper, you may wish to have a thymol cabinet built.

In a thymol cabinet, thymol crystals are placed on a metal floor and their fumes rise to permeate the paper laid on racks above. A 40-watt bulb is burned in the cabinet for three hours daily to volatilize the crystals, and it must be strategically placed to prevent the metal floor from overheating, or vapors will recondense and may form oily spots on paper.

Air all storage areas periodically, particularly in houses closed for any length of time.

Restoration

■

The science of paper restoration is among the most complex of conservation forms.

Among problems conservators and restorers frequently treat are mold and the mottled brown stains known as foxing, which may result from a damp environment or from the original chemical processing of the paper.

Foxing and many other stains require various techniques of washing and bleaching. Mold on dry paper can sometimes be brushed off, except on charcoals and pastels, after which an hour of exposure to ultraviolet or sunlight will kill any mold residue.

Mold is also killed by sterilization with brief, repeated exposure to thymol fumes or orthophenylphenol crystals.

Adhesive stains may be ameliorated with solvents, but invariably brown stain traces remain.

Buckled, creased, or wrinkled paper is treated in a humidity chamber, an airtight container or box in which paper is placed on a fiberglass screen above a tray of cold water. When the paper absorbs enough moisture to become limp, it is weighted with plate glass between top and bottom layers of tissue and blotting paper.

Paper should never be ironed!

When paper is torn, a special stylus will draw the ends of severed fibers outward from the break until they meet or overlap on the tear line. Once aligned, the tear is reinforced from behind with Japan tissue affixed with a small amount of water-soluble rice or wheat starch paste, weighted, and checked frequently to assure that the paste doesn't penetrate the paper and adhere to the top blotting layer.

Special powdered erasers are used on soot and dirt stains, and acetone on oil and grease.

Weakened paper may be reinforced by sizing or deacidifying, and soaked paper is dried on blotters but not weighted.

Whenever damage or deterioration is present in paper, a conservator should be consulted. Attempts to reverse or eliminate problems without professional advice run the risk of creating major casualties.

To find a paper restorer, contact the Guild of Bookworkers or the American Institute for Conservation of Historic and Artistic Works (for addresses, consult "Sources and Services" in the back of the book).

Books

■

Mass-production techniques of papermaking that came into general use during the Industrial Revolution and persisted for one hundred years, until 1950, have resulted in the disintegration of millions of embrittled books, which are being consumed by the acid byproducts of alum compounds. They are consequently literally disintegrating into powder.

In this country's major libraries, approximately 25 percent of the books (and 40 percent of those in research collections) are now or soon will be too fragile to touch.

Conservators, libraries, and government have tried to generate a concerted effort to microfilm more than three million volumes, but twice that many are far beyond hope.

An individual volume can be deacidified if its paper has some remaining stability, but the time and labor demanded for each book make this a thoroughly impractical and invalid approach, as costs per book skyrocket beyond two hundred dollars.

The National Library of Canada is now using a liquefied-gas deacidifying system to treat up to 150,000 volumes annually, and the

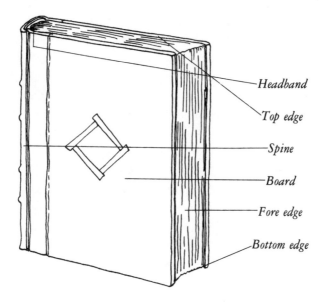

Headband

Top edge

Spine

Board

Fore edge

Bottom edge

U.S. Library of Congress plans to open a plant by 1990 to treat a million books a year, but again, these mass treatments will preserve only books with a viable degree of remaining strength. A good many more have already been lost or soon will be as time runs out.

*E*nvironment

■

In addition to inherent acid content, other factors that adversely affect books are light, heat, moisture, environmental pollutants, and infestation.

Books should be kept in a constant environment, where light sources are filtered and shaded, and exposure to all light is minimal.

The ideal climate for books is 60 to 68 percent relative humidity. The lower end of these scales is preferable.

A very dry climate will cause brittleness in leather, paper, and vellum, and excessive moisture loosens the adhesives used in bookbinding. Moisture in the presence of inadequate ventilation invites mold.

Proper air flow can be provided by leaving a space of at least an inch both behind the shelved books and behind the bookcase, between its back and the wall, especially if it is an outside wall.

Shelves should be cut and placed with a space of one inch at the back of each shelf, separating it from the back of the bookcase.

If shelves are fixed and cannot be cut, drill one-inch holes along the back of the shelf, three inches apart.

Bookcases with glass doors are extremely difficult to ventilate effectively, and are considered potentially hazardous for book storage.

Handling and Storage

∎

To remove a book from the shelf, push back the books on either side of it several inches, grip the spine firmly, and pull it out. If you make a practice of pulling the book by the top of the binding, where the headband is glued to the paper, you will loosen the adhesive and may one day find you have removed the binding and left the rest of the book on the shelf.

Alternatively, if there is enough space between the top of the book and the shelf above, reach over the book to the fore edge, which is the side where the pages open, and pull it gently toward you.

Always support the bottom edge of any book that is large or heavy.

Don't pack books very tightly on a shelf. Not only do they need

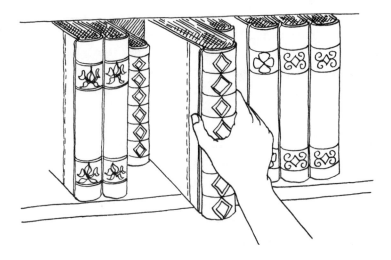

*To remove a book from the shelf, push back the books
on either side of it several inches.*

■

sufficient air circulation to breathe, but crushing them will destroy the
bindings.

Conversely, if they are arranged too loosely, and lean at an angle, the
binding's structure will be stressed enough to break it down.

If there aren't enough books to fill a shelf, place them comfortably
at one end, and use bookends or wooden blocks to give correct support
while keeping the remaining space vacant.

Stand books upright on the shelf. Don't stand them on the fore edge
(the opening side) or the spine will weaken and loosen.

If a book is too thick or heavy to be stood upright, lay it flat, but
don't stack more than two or three books atop one another or the fore
edges will sag.

Turned-down corners, unless they are embrittled, should be turned back or dust will accumulate in the open space provided. Don't unfold the corners of pages that have been turned in the book's original manufacture, however, as they have been folded over before the pages were cut, and are part of the structure's design and dimension.

If books have metal corners, clasps, or other attachments, separate them from the books on either side by an acid-free board to prevent the metal from damaging neighboring volumes.

If the bookcase has metal grooves in its sides to raise and lower shelves, place an acid-free board next to the hardware to prevent the book at the end of the row from being damaged.

Bookshelves should be constructed of hardwood, not softwood, and never of metal, which may corrode.

Loose spines (backs) and boards (side panels) of a book should be

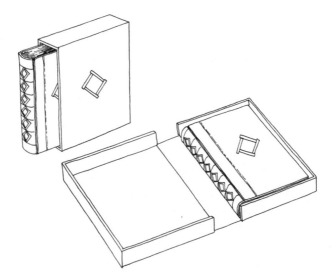

Valued books should be stored in archival slipcases, boxes, or portfolios.

■

wrapped with soft cloth tape and tied. Don't use string or rubber bands.

If the book's entire structure has come apart or is near grave disrepair, protect it with a wrapper of acid-free lightweight board or acid-free paper.

Valued books should be stored in archival slipcases, boxes, or portfolios. Don't store them in plastic covers, brown (acidic) paper covers, or with any metal attachments, such as paper clips attached to pages.

Cleaning

■

To dust a book after removing it from the shelf, hold it firmly by the fore edge, supporting it between your waist and elbow if its weight requires it.

With a shaving brush, or a brush of the same approximate size and texture, brush along the top edge, away from the headband (the bound end).

If dust has fallen between the pages, which may happen if the paper has cockled and is no longer lying flat, if a page has been turned down, or if separating markers have been left between pages, brush out the dirt page by page with a sable or similarly textured brush.

Dust the spine and boards (back and sides) with a soft cloth.

Never remove dust by knocking books against each other.

When dusting books, wash your hands often to avoid transferring dirt from one book to another.

While dusting, examine books for mold and insect damage.

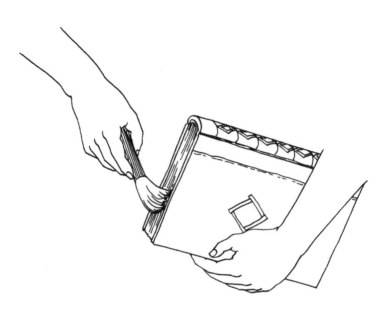

With a soft brush, dust the book's top edge, brushing away from the headband.

Silverfish, book lice, and woodworm thrive on mold and can mutilate both paper and leather. Given the opportunity, rats and mice will consume starch and gelatin adhesives, and ravage the rest of the book by shredding it for nest material.

Treat leather bindings once or twice a year with leather preservatives, which both clean and protect fine bindings. Many bookbinders recommend Talas Leather Protector™, which neutralizes acids caused by air pollution, replaces natural salts that are used in the tanning process but are later washed away, and protects against mold and mildew; and Talas Leather Dressing™, which revives leather and helps to maintain its original beauty, luster, and suppleness.

Consult a book conservator if any sign of infestation is present.

*R*estoration and Repair

■

To be on the safe side, no book repair should be initiated without the advice of a conservator.

Under no circumstances, even as a temporary measure, use adhesive tape such as Scotch Tape on books or on any paper products. They will leave dark, permanent stains.

Leather, in particular, requires sound conservatorial care or advice. In time, invariably its natural oils are lost and it becomes prone to cracking.

High relative humidity (over 70 percent) may generate a powdery decomposition known as leather rot.

Conservators have developed a variety of products to replace lost oils and fats, most of which are neat's-foot oil based, with wax and mold inhibitor added. Petroleum jelly has been used but is less preferred because it is absorbed extremely slowly, and treated leather remains sticky for a prolonged period of time.

Petroleum jelly is the dressing of choice for leather rot, however, and it seems to reduce the accelerating rate of decomposition when that condition is present.

Some dressings have been specifically formulated for a defined environment. In the United States, the New York Public Library formula has been very successful.

Experienced bookbinders and restorers will rebind, deacidify, and protectively box your valued books to preserve them safely for many generations of bibliophiles to come.

To locate a conservator or restorer, contact the Guild of Bookworkers or the American Institute for Conservation of Historic and Artistic Works (see back of book, "Sources and Services," for their addresses).

Photographs

■

Photography is a relatively recent process, barely 150 years old, and while not everyone owns an oil painting or an Aubusson rug, virtually everyone owns and cherishes at least a few photographs.

The first photograph was produced in France in 1839 by L.-J.-M. Daguerre and J. N. Niepce, and until 1860 millions more were made using their process. Daguerreotypes, as they were known, produced a direct image on a copper support thinly coated with silver. The image appeared as a positive only at certain angles of light, and otherwise appeared as a negative or as a reflector.

Most daguerreotypes were sixth-plate-sized portraits 2½ by 3¼ inches, and seldom were larger than whole-plate size, or 6½ by 8½. They were commonly covered with glass and displayed in a decorative case.

In 1841, William H. F. Talbot patented the calotype process. Known also as the talbotype, this was the first paper negative process, on which today's positive-negative printing system is based. Many landscape and architectural talbotypes were produced in France and England, but very few in America.

In 1850, Louis-Désiré Blanquart-Evrard introduced albumen paper, on which most surviving nineteenth-century photographs are printed. These very thin paper prints were nearly always mounted on stiff cardboard backings.

In 1851, architect Scott Archer coated glass plate with liquid collodion and produced the first wet-plate collodion photographs, called ambrotypes. This process on the then new albumen paper offered much finer tone and detail. Ambrotypes were mounted in the same manner as daguerreotypes, but were easily distinguished because they appeared as positive images in all angles of light.

In 1856, Hamilton Smith patented the ferrotype process, using a thin sheet of iron as a support instead of glass, and although tin is not used in the process, these soon became and continue to be known as tintypes. Itinerant photographers soon made millions of tintypes throughout America. These direct positives were usually packaged in similar decorative display cases as daguerreotypes and ambrotypes.

In 1871, Dr. R. L. Maddox developed the process still in use today, substituting gelatin for collodion, on a sensitive dry plate. Photographic papers continue to be refined, but from 1890 until now the photographic process has remained substantially the same.

*E*nvironment

■

Photographs react extremely sensitively to their environment. They may embrittle, curl, buckle, fade, dissolve, discolor, fox, tarnish, stain, grow mold, or attract insects.

Moisture adversely affects all photographic materials. To ensure their permanence, keep humidity at 40 to 50 percent and temperature at 70 degrees Fahrenheit.

In areas of high pollution, heavy traffic, or existing industry, use air conditioning and air purification devices. All fumes, whether from gasoline, household heating systems, chemicals, paints, cosmetics, inks, or varnish, speed the oxidation process of both paper and film.

The blue and ultraviolet rays prevalent in daylight fade dyes, break down gelatin fibers, and convert other chemical substances to colored compounds. These chemical changes, once under way, continue to occur even after daylight ends and the light source is removed.

Calotype images are held directly on and within the fibers of the paper support and are extremely photosensitive. Store them in the dark at all times.

The dyes in virtually all color photographs are considered unstable, although some Lumière Autochrome transparencies (c. 1920) are still visually vivid. Most color images, including those contemporarily produced, are fugitive and fade dramatically. Expose them to as little light as possible, and then preferably to tungsten light. Store color photographs in a cool, dry, acid-free environment at all times.

Storage

Store photographs in the rooms you live in, where fluctuations in temperature and relative humidity are minimized, instead of in attics or basements.

Most of the photograph albums we treasure for historical and sentimental reasons are accelerating decay of the pictures they contain, because of the low-grade paper and highly acidic adhesives and plastic separators used in their construction. Photographs in these albums would be better off stored in a cardboard box, a pronouncement that will be well received by anyone who feels guilty about their boxes of unmounted snapshots.

The most harmful album is the most common one, the magnetic album in which photographs adhere to sticky, plastic-covered cardboard pages. The cardboard gives off peroxides that stain the whites of both color and black-and-white prints, while the plastic gives off gases that attack the photographic image. The adhesives transfer to the print, which ultimately bonds to the page and cannot be removed without tearing.

These aren't the only damaging types of album. The black backing paper in almost all older albums gives off gases that are devastating to photographic images, as are rubber cement, animal glues, and mucilage.

To cover photographs, use only nonpolyvinyl chloride plastics, such as polyester (Mylar™), polyethylene, polypropylene, triacetate, and Tyvek™.

Special archival photograph albums are the best protection for photographs, and their cost is very little more than that of the popular but destructive albums in wide use.

Keep negatives, slides, prints, and transparencies in envelopes, sleeves, folders, albums, or boxes, or in steel, stainless steel, or aluminum cabinets designed specifically for archival storage of photographic materials.

Separate each stored item with acid-free interleaving sheets of treated paper, or nonpolyvinyl chloride plastic, but not with glassine or kraft paper.

Don't store them in wood, particleboard, pressboard, or cardboard, whose fumes attack photographs.

Don't write on photographs with either ballpoint or felt-tip pens, which tend to bleed, but with a No. 2 pencil instead.

All light is destructive to photographs. If you plan to hang a color photograph on the wall or frame it for your bureau, have an extra print made. While the light is causing your treasured image to disappear rapidly, you'll have a backup copy stored carefully away whose color and image quality are intact.

Processed prints are necessarily acidic, usually with a pH of approximately 5.5. Alkaline papers with a high calcium carbonate content take up acidity, and the boundary beyond which prints are at risk of damage from acid loss has not yet been clearly established. To be on the safe side, don't store photographs and photographic materials in acid-free paper or near other acid-free products with a pH factor of over 8.5.

Developing

Avoid instant developing labs, especially for color prints. Often the prints are not properly or thoroughly washed, and a residue of chemicals may promote disintegration.

Framing

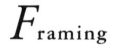

For display, frame photographs in aluminum, stainless steel, silver or acrylic (Plexiglas, Lucite, Permacryl) instead of in wood frames, whose acidic properties migrate to the photographs. Back frames with acid-free mat board, preferably slightly alkaline (up to a factor of 8.5), which will help resist and protect against environmental pollutants. Ventilation is vital for photographs. The back of the frame must not be sealed.

Use a separating strip or an acid-free mat to maintain space between the photograph and the cover glass or acrylic to prevent ferrotyping. This is a surface change that can be produced on prints by pressure contact with the cover glass and that results in increased high gloss on the photograph's surface.

Prints should be hinged, but if you must mount them, use photographic dry mounting tissue. A preferred alternative is acid-free corner mounts, which can be cut from Permalife™ or other neutral paper envelopes. Attach with an adhesive such as polyvinyl acetate.

Restoration

■

A photographic restorer can clean prints, films, plates, and transparencies, can remove stains, discoloration, and fungus, and can intensify faded images and flatten creases. All restoration involves elaborate chemical processes, and only an established photographic laboratory that specializes in restoration should handle these problems.

The image on daguerreotypes and on some ambrotypes is so fragile that no cleaning method is recommended as 100 percent safe. If a photographic conservator advises that they should not be worked on, be sure they are properly sealed in their cases, and handle them as seldom as possible.

To locate a conservator or restorer of photographs, contact a photography museum, an art museum with an extensive photography collection, or a university with a photography department (see "Sources and Services").

Silver and Other Metals

■

Although we tend to think of metals as durable and indestructible, metal surfaces are in fact easily scratched and worn away, corroding at a rate dependent on the metal's compounds and the conditions to which it is exposed.

Even the routine polishing of nonferrous metals removes a small amount of metal each time.

Because environmental pollutants corrode metal, air-conditioning and air-filtering systems help maintain a beneficial environment, retarding both corrosion and oxidation. The ideal climatic condition for metal is 70 degrees Fahrenheit and 45 to 50 percent relative humidity.

Stored metals should be wrapped in polyethylene or acid-free tissue. Don't wrap them in plastic, or condensation may form.

Metal polishes are acidic and tarnish-inducing, and thus must be completely wiped off after each use. To polish or dry, use very soft cloths; the texture of a linen dish towel, for instance, is far too abrasive and will tend to scratch and remove metal surfaces. Bonded, all-purpose kitchen cloths, such as Handi Wipes™, work well, as do

Silver tarnishes from exposure to chloride salts or sulfur compounds.

■

recycled flannel nightgowns, cloth diapers, and T-shirts.

After polishing, dry metals gently but thoroughly, because the chlorides and other chemicals present in most urban water are also corrosive.

Always use separate polishing cloths for silver, brass, and copper.

Silver

■

Silver, like gold, is chemically inactive. It doesn't oxidize when exposed to air, but tarnishes from exposure to chloride salts or sulfur compounds.

Among sources of the latter are pollution, perspiration, egg yolks, olives, peas, vinegar, fruit, flowers, perfumes, latex paints, natural gas, adhesives, and sea air, all of which promote rapid tarnishing.

Empty silver salt dishes after each use, or the salt will pit them, causing permanent damage. If you use silver candy, nut, or serving dishes, wash and dry them thoroughly afterward to remove all possible damaging food residue.

To keep the silver looking lustrous, our great-grandmothers wiped it daily with plate rags. These were made by boiling soft cloth, preferably the tops of old cotton stockings, in a mixture of new milk and hartshorn powder. The rags were then dropped into cold water and dried by the fire.

Today, we advise you to polish silver no more than absolutely necessary, and then with the purest, mildest available product, such as calcium carbonate and olive oil, which is nontoxic and can be wiped off when dry, or Goddard's™. If a commercial product's ingredients aren't listed, write the manufacturer. If they won't tell you, try another product and another letter.*

Avoid silver polishes containing silica, ammonia, or tarnish inhibitors, all of which are highly abrasive, as are most dip cleaners.

Alternatively, jeweler's rouge, diatomaceous earth, or calcium carbonate (whiting or precipitated chalk) may be mixed with denatured alcohol and distilled water for as effective a silver polish as you could purchase. In formulating a silver polish, add only small amounts of liquid, just enough to make a paste. If using denatured alcohol and distilled water, use them in equal amounts.

Never use all-purpose metal polishes, as their formula is far too harsh.

On intricately worked silver detail, use a jeweler's silver brush or the softest available natural bristle toothbrush to reach crevices.

Be particularly gentle with Sheffield and other plate, or you may totally remove the thin coating of silver and expose the copper or other metal underneath.

---

* Ethanol and sulfur compounds, sometimes used in silver polishes, have been linked to cancer. Do not inhale their fumes, and protect your hands with rubber gloves while using them. Dispose of both materials and containers as hazardous waste.

Use a soft, natural-bristle toothbrush to reach crevices when polishing intricately worked silver detail.

■

For silver storage, antitarnish strips are available that retard tarnish most effectively, as do small camphor squares. Place them in your silver closet or chest, but be sure not to let them come into direct contact with silver.

Don't wrap silver in felt or chamois leather. Both are sources of hydrogen sulfide, a strong tarnish inducer. Never wrap plated silver in newspaper. Printer's ink will act in time to remove the plating.

Copper and Brass

■

Copper and its alloys, including brass, respond to simple polishes whose base is either rottenstone, jeweler's rouge, diatomaceous earth, or calcium carbonate (whiting or precipitated chalk) made to a thick paste with denatured alcohol and distilled water.

Many commercial cleaners contain acids or chlorides, which quickly start new corrosion and may pit the metal, as does salt mixed with lemon juice or vinegar.

Copper pots used regularly will most likely need to be retinned at least every five years, or when the lining begins to wear away. Otherwise, toxic amounts of copper may leach into the food, altering the taste or turning it greenish.

You will need to retin more frequently if you cook acid foods, such as tomato sauce, in your copper pots, because many acids interact with the tin to promote its breakdown.

Use a low flame under copper to avoid blistering the tin, and clean lined copper pots or unlined bowls as you would Teflon™, using a nonabrasive pad or sponge.

Use only plastic, Teflon, or wooden utensils to stir with or serve from copper.

If you choose to lacquer copper or brass, use only a specially formulated synthetic lacquer, such as Incralac™.

Bronze

Don't try to wash or polish bronze. Chlorides or other chemicals present in the water may instigate the rapid corrosion known as bronze disease and, furthermore, polish is likely to remove the patina.

Instead, simply dust bronze regularly and lightly with a very soft cloth. Be sure to remove all traces of dust, which may otherwise attract moisture and thus precipitate bronze disease as well.

Pewter

■

On pewter, many people prefer to leave a dull gray patina.

If you wish to polish pewter, do so gently, with jeweler's rouge or rottenstone mixed with mineral oil or denatured alcohol. Add just enough mineral oil or denatured alcohol to the jeweler's rouge to form a soft paste.

Treat Britannia ware in the same manner, as its base of tin, usually with antimony and copper, is the same as that of pewter, although Britannia metal is much harder than pewter.

Pewter is often displayed on oak but shouldn't be stored in a closed oak cabinet or drawer, because the organic acids in oak or in untreated, unseasoned woods promote pewter deterioration.

Gold, Gilt, and Ormolu

■

Gold, like silver, is chemically inactive, and is the only metal not affected by moisture, acids, or oxygen. It doesn't require polishing because it won't tarnish.

Be sure never to polish silver gilt (gold thinly layered on silver) or ormolu (gold thinly layered on copper or brass). You will remove the gold and expose the metal underneath, which then will tarnish. If this occurs, the gold can sometimes be restored, but this is a very expensive process.

If you own ormolu candlesticks, use glass wax-protectors to keep wax from dripping on them, and be careful not to polish the gold linings in bowls or salt dishes, or these thin layers will quickly vanish.

Restoration

∎

If you have any reservation about cleaning and/or polishing metals due to excessive corrosion or other wear, contact a metals conservator. Extreme caution is required for disfigured or neglected metal objects. Additionally, with any plated object there is always the danger of separating the layers by using chemical cleaners. Metal conservators have the tools and techniques to identify an object's components and preserve or restore its surface and appearance, whereas inappropriate home treatments could lead to disaster.

To locate a conservator, contact a museum whose collections include objects of the same metal composition as those you wish to have restored or repaired (see state museum listings under "Sources and Services"), or contact the American Institute for Conservation of Historic and Artistic Works (see list of associations in the same chapter).

eramics

■

Ceramics include a wide variety of baked materials, which can be divided into two general categories. The first includes low-fired pottery and earthenware—Indian pottery, faience, majolica, delft—and soft-paste porcelain—Derby, Chelsea, Mennecy, Worcester, bone china—which are porous and tend to be fragile. The second category embraces high-fired pottery or stoneware—celadon, English stoneware and creamware, unglazed Wedgwood basalt and jasperware—and hard-paste, true porcelain—Chinese, Meissen, Sevres, unglazed biscuit-ware—which are nonporous and durable.

Environment

■

Although the rate of environmental damage to ceramics is slower than to other organic materials, they are nonetheless affected by excessive and prolonged heat and moisture. Under these conditions, glazes tend

*Excessive or prolonged heat or moisture may cause ceramic glazes to develop
a pattern of small lines and cracks known as crazing.*

■

to develop a pattern of small cracks known as crazing, and unglazed,
porous objects may absorb moisture, resulting in swelling or leaching
of components.

Keep ceramics in dry areas, away from cooling and heating sources.

Storage and Handling

■

Stack plates together only if they are the same shape and size, and never
with a larger plate on top of a smaller one.

Interleave them with felt pads, thickly folded tissue, or bubble wrap. Deep soup plates will need an extra-thick cushion. Never stack cups or bowls.

The footing on ceramic objects is often unglazed, and rough bases may scratch other ceramic pieces if left unpadded.

Ceramic bases may also scratch polished surfaces. Protect them with cork, felt, or chamois mats, even on marble or stone. Mats are especially important under all flower containers. Otherwise condensation from the water in which the flowers stand may cause stains either on the ceramic or on the surface on which it is placed.

To lift a ceramic object, support it well in both hands. Don't pick up any piece, including a lid, by a handle, spout, or by any appendage or restored part. Lift plates and bowls from beneath, not by the rim.

To hang ceramic plates or platters, protect glaze from metal stains by strips of felt under the clips, or humid conditions may result in irreversible metal stains on the ceramic surface.

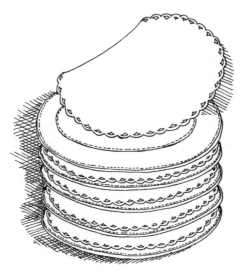

Interleave plates with felt pads to protect them from scratching and chipping.

■

Cleaning

Dust ceramics with a soft cloth. Don't immerse unglazed, low-fired pottery, earthenware, or terra-cotta. It may swell, or components may be leached. Chemicals or dirt in water may stain. Don't immerse objects with gold or silver decoration, or with repairs. Metallic decoration may wash off; repairs will come unglued. Never wash repaired pieces in the dishwasher.

Wash valuable pieces by hand. If an object is nonporous and has had no repairs, wash it in lukewarm water and mild detergent. Rinse with clear water. Don't use strong detergent, ammonia, washing soda, scouring pads, cleaning powders, or soap, which leaves a smeary film.

The chemicals in dishwasher detergents may damage or remove the decoration or pattern on china that is overglazed. Overglazed pieces are put through the kiln both before and after decoration. Their patterns may be slightly raised and usually appear less glossy then the rest of the piece. Gold is always overglazed.

Washing ceramics in or with aluminum pans, or placing them in contact with aluminum in the dishwasher, produces irreversible, gray, pencil-like lines on most china.

Don't let staining foods or liquids, including tea and coffee, stand on or in ceramics longer than necessary. Even glazed ceramics may tend to stain. Tea and coffee stains may be removed with a small amount of baking soda on a wet dishcloth.

If crazed or crackled glaze becomes discolored, it is sometimes possible to restore it by applying 20-volume hydrogen peroxide. Then wash and rinse well.

Don't put warm or hot ceramics into cold water, or cold ceramics into hot water. Sudden temperature changes may cause pieces to break.

Water that is too hot may cause crazing lines.

Ormolu mounts on ceramics must not be allowed to get wet.

Restoration and Repairs

■

Before attempting repairs on any important object, consult a conservator, and use only conservation suppliers' adhesives.

Repair items only when the edges of a break are clean and dry, using as thin a glue line as possible. Missing segments may be reconstructed from plaster of Paris or other traditional material, or a conservator might recommend molding or casting parts from a similar item.

Many collectors and conservators prefer to leave reconstructed areas untinted. Otherwise, artists' acrylic colors are generally used, but replicating color, design, and a matte or gloss finish should be left to a trained, skilled, and knowledgeable specialist. To locate a conservator, contact a museum with a ceramics collection or the American Institute for Conservation of Historic and Artistic Works.

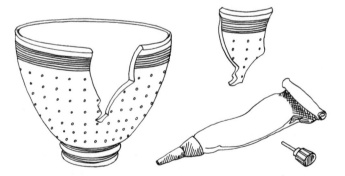

Repair ceramics with a thin glue line on a clean, dry break.

■

*G*lass

■

Glass is made by fusing silica (sand) with alkalis (ash, potash). Metallic oxides may be added for color, lime for clarity and stability, or lead to produce crystal.

The mixture is then heated until liquefied, when it is formed (blown) or molded, and finally cooled to harden.

If the proportion of ingredients is correct, the glass is stable, durable, and insensitive to moisture.

*E*nvironment

■

Glass, like ceramic, tends to be resistant to environmental chemicals, but sudden and severe temperature changes may cause breakage, and excessive, prolonged heat or dampness may cause a milky, cloudy appearance.

Storage and Handling

■

Store individual glass objects separately and don't put glass items inside each other.

If glasses are inadvertently stacked and become stuck, fill the top glass with cold water and immerse the lower one in hot tap water to separate them.

Pad the feet of glass objects when possible.

Don't store any glassware unless it is completely dry. Store glasses upright, especially crystal glasses, whose rims are their weakest points.

Don't crowd glass objects in storage; leaving space around each item lessens the risk of damage.

Don't lift glass objects by the rim or by an extending part; support an object's full weight by the base.

Don't use bare metal mounts for displaying glass, since metal may scratch or stain it.

Cleaning

■

Wash glass in warm water and a mild detergent. Don't use soap, which will leave a visible film. Add a little ammonia for extra shine.

Allow glass to drain dry, or dry it with a soft, lintless cloth.

Don't put cold glass into hot water, or warm glass into water that is very cold.

Don't immerse glass with gold or silver ornamentations, or wash it in hot water, ammonia, harsh soaps, or dishwasher detergents.

To wash delicate glass objects, slip them into the water sideways.

Immersing them in hot water bottom first may produce cracks or splits.

When washing parts of a chandelier, or a lamp or candlestick with crystal prisms, be sure the parts are thoroughly dry before reassembly, or hooks and wires may rust and corrode.

Glass containers on which there are dried food, liquid, or other organic or chemical deposits should be filled with a mixture of water, detergent, and laundry water softener, and left to soak overnight. Then remove the residue with a bottle brush. If the bottoms of glass decanters become cloudy, mix sand and denatured alcohol in the decanter and shake it vigorously to make the glass sparkle.

Dry a narrow-mouthed container by inserting absorbent material, which absorbs moisture and releases it outside the container.

■

If the container's mouth is too narrow for a brush and stains persist, and if the glass is not extremely thin and fragile, add a handful or more of air rifle (BB) shot, and gently roll it back and forth by slow and careful tilting until deposits are removed. Rinse with distilled water to prevent further deposits.

To dry a narrow-mouthed container, tightly roll and insert into it a piece of absorbent paper or cloth, long enough so that it reaches the container's bottom, while half of it hangs out over the edge of the mouth. It will slowly but finally dry, as the inserted material absorbs moisture and releases it outside the container.

Some cloudy stains on glass can be removed by filling the object with four parts water and one part ammonia and leaving it to soak for a day or overnight. Remove alkaline deposit stains on glass with white vinegar.

Restoration and Repairs

■

Incorrect proportions of components in manufacture and resultant chemical or physical changes may lead glass to deteriorate and lose stability, resulting in crizzling or in weeping glass.

Crizzling is evidenced by an extensive, dried-out pattern of fine lines and cracks, similar to crazing in ceramics. Tiny shards along these fissures may progressively splinter off.

Weeping glass noticeably absorbs moisture in its surface layer, but drying it out will cause shrinkage and crizzling.

These conditions are irreversible, but are slowed by a stable environment with 45 to 50 percent relative humidity.

Repairs to broken glass should be made with specifically formulated adhesives. For proper adhesion, broken edges may need to be roughened, and drying is often a lengthy process because the meeting surfaces are nonporous.

A hundred years ago, a cement to repair china or glass was made by dissolving an ounce of gum mastic in a quantity of highly rectified spirits of wine. Next, an ounce of isinglass was softened in warm water and then dissolved in rum or brandy until it formed a thick jelly. The gum mastic and isinglass were then added to an ounce of finely powdered gum ammoniac. This mixture was placed in an earthen pipkin and kept in a warm place until thoroughly incorporated and then it was set aside in a glass phial or jar.

To use the cement, a small piece of hardened material was broken off and melted in a silver teaspoon held over a candle. Fortunately, today's methods are far simpler.

Two-part resins are recommended. They are fast drying, but may become ineffective in high (70 to 80 percent) relative humidity.

Nicks or chips in rims or bases can be sanded smooth with 00 sandpaper, preferably by a conservator or by a glazier.

To locate a conservator, contact a museum with a glass collection, or the American Institute for Conservation of Historic and Artistic Works. For museum-quality American glass, contact the American Ceramics Arts Society. (See "Sources and Services.")

Sources and Services

■

These listings do not represent an endorsement by the authors.

Associations

■

American Art Pottery Association
(AAPA)
Tom Layman, Secretary
9825 Upton Circle
Bloomington, MN 55431
(612) 884-2604

American Association of Dealers
in Ancient, Oriental and
Primitive Art (AADAOPA)
122 E. 93rd St.
New York, NY 10128
(212) 722-1099

American Association of Museums
(AAM)
1225 I St. NW
Washington, DC 20005
(202) 289-1818

American Ceramics Arts Society
(ACAS)
% William Goodman
1775 Broadway
Suite 2404
New York, NY 10019
(212) 586-1760

American Federation of Arts
(AFA)
41 E. 65th St.
New York, NY 10021
(212) 988-7700

American Historical Print Collectors Society (AHPCS)
25 W. 43rd St.
New York, NY 10036
(914) 795-5266

American Institute for Conservation of Historic and Artistic Works (AIC)
3545 Williamsburg Lane NW
Washington DC 20009
(202) 364-1036

American Numismatic Society
Broadway and 156th St.
New York, NY 10032
(212) 234-3130

American Philatelic Society (APS)
Box 800
100 Oakwood Ave.
State College, PA 16803
(814) 237-3803

American Society of Appraisers (ASA)
Box 17265
Washington, DC 20041
and
535 Herndon Parkway
Herndon, VA 22070
(703) 478-2228

Antiquarian Booksellers Association of America (ABAA)
50 Rockefeller Plaza
New York, NY 10020
(212) 757-9395

Antiquarian Booksellers Association of Canada (ABAC)
Box 863, Station F
Toronto, ON M4Y 2N7
Canada
(416) 871-7859

Antique Appraisers Association of America (AAAA)
11361 Garden Grove Blvd.
Garden Grove, CA 92643
(714) 530-7090

Antique Dealers Association of California (ADACA)
722 Bay St.
San Francisco, CA 94109
(415) 474-4027

Antiques Dealers' Association of America Inc. (ADAA)
P.O. Box 335
Green Farms, CT 06436
(203) 259-3844

Appraisers Association of America (AAA)
60 E. 42nd St.
New York, NY 10165
(212) 867-9775

Archaeological Institute of America (AIOA)
Box 1901
Kenmore Station
Boston, MA 02215
(617) 353-9361

Art and Antique Dealers League of America (AADLA)
353 E. 78th St.
Suite 19A
New York, NY 10021
(212) 879-7558

Art Dealers Association of America, Inc. (ADAA)
575 Madison Ave.
New York, NY 10022
(212) 940-8590

Art Deco Society (ADS)
145 Hudson St.
New York, NY 10013
(212) 925-4946

Art Deco Society of California (ADSCA)
109 Minna St.
Suite 399
San Francisco, CA 94105
(415) 552-3326

Associated Antique Dealers of America (AADA)
Box 8854
Indianapolis, IN 46208

Association of International Photography Art Dealers (AIPAD)
93 Standish Rd.
Hillsdale, NJ 07642
(201) 664-4600

Association of Professional Art Advisors (APAA)
Box 2485
New York, NY 10163
(212) 645-7320

Berkshire County Antique Dealers Association (BCADA)
R.D. 1, Box 1

Sheffield, MA 01257
(413) 229-2628

Canadian Antique Dealers Association (CADA)
Box 517, Station K
Toronto, ON M4P 2E0
Canada
(416) 222-0666

Canadian Conservation Institute
1030 Innes Rd.
Ottawa, ON K1A OM8
Canada
(416) 998-3721

Connecticut Antique Dealers Association (CADA)
% George Gorton
Box 367
Middlefield, CT 06455
(203) 349-8697

Decorative Arts Trust (DAT)
106 Bainbridge
Philadelphia, PA 19147
(215) 627-2859

Early American Industries Association (EAIA)
Box 2128
Empire State Plaza Station
Albany, NY 12220

The Ephemera Society of America, Inc. (ESA)
Box 943
Hillsboro, NH 03244
(603) 464-5413

Gemological Institute of America
  (GIA)
1180 Ave. of the Americas
New York, NY 10036
(212) 944-5900

Glass Art Society (GAS)
20300 N. Greenway
Southfield, MI 48076
(313) 357-0783

Guild of Bookworkers
521 Fifth Ave.
New York, NY 10175
(212) 757-6454

Indian Arts and Crafts Association
  (IACA)
4215 Lead SE
Albuquerque, NM 97108
(505) 265-9149

International Center of Medieval
  Art (ICMA)
The Cloisters
Fort Tryon Park
New York, NY 10040
(212) 923-3700

International Chinese Snuff Bottle
  Society (ICSBS)
2601 N. Charles St.
Baltimore, MD 21218
(301) 467-9400

International Fabric Care Institute
12251 Tech Rd.

Silver Spring, MD 20904
(301) 622-1900

International Fine Print Dealers
  Association (IFPDA)
485 Madison Ave.
New York, NY 10022
(212) 935-6020

International Society of Appraisers
  (ISA)
Box 726
Hoffman Estates, IL 60195
(312) 882-0706

International Society of Fine Arts
  Appraisers (ISFAA)
Box 280
River Forest, IL 60305
(312) 848-3340

Japan Society (JS)
333 E. 47th St.
New York, NY 10017
(212) 832-1155

Maine Antique Dealers Associa-
  tion (MADA)
% The Beehive
Box 41
Alfred, ME 04002
(207) 324-0990

Manuscript Society (MS)
350 N. Niagara St.
Burbank, CA 91505
(818) 845-3011

Minnesota Antique Dealers Association (MADA)
3801 Pillsbury South
Minneapolis, MN 55409
(612) 291-2400

National Antique and Art Dealers Association of America (NAADAA)
32 E. 66th St.
New York, NY 10021
(212) 517-5760

National Association of Dealers in Antiques (NADA)
5859 N. Main Rd.
Rockford, IL 61103
(815) 877-4282

National Association of Watch and Clock Collectors (NAWCC)
514 Poplar St.
Columbia, PA 17512
(717) 684-8261

National Customs Brokers and Forwarders of America (NCBFAA)
5 World Trade Center
Suite 9273
New York, NY 10048
(212) 432-0050

National Fire Protection Association (NFPA)
60 Batterymarch St.
Boston, MA 02110
(617) 770-3000

National Trust for Historic Preservation (NTHP)
1785 Massachusetts Ave. NW
Washington, DC 20036
(202) 673-4000

Neighborhood Cleaners Association
116 E. 27th St.
New York, NY 10016
(212) 684-0945

New England Appraisers Association (NEAA)
104 Charles St.
Boston, MA 02114
(617) 523-6272
and
5 Gill Terr.
Ludlow, VT 05149
(802) 228-7444

New Hampshire Antiques Dealers Association (NHADA)
RFD 1, Box 3056
Tilton, NH 03276
(603) 286-4908

Professional Art Dealers Association of Canada (PADAC)
111 Elizabeth St.
Suite 1100
Toronto, ON M5G 1P7
Canada
(416) 979-1276

Professional Numismatists Guild
  % Paul Koppenhaver
  Box 430
  Van Nuys, CA 91408
  (818) 781-1764

Professional Picture Framers Association (PPFA)
  POB 7655
  4305 Sarellen Rd.
  Richmond, VA 23231
  (804) 226-0430

Vermont Antique Dealers Association
  55 Allen St.
  Rutland, VT 05701
  (802) 773-8630

Victorian Society of America
  219 S. 6th St.
  Philadelphia, PA 19106
  (215) 627-4252

Museums

■

Alabama
  Birmingham Museum of Art
  Huntsville Museum of Art
  Montgomery Museum of Fine
    Arts

Alaska
  Anchorage Museum of History
    and Art
  Visual Art Center of Alaska,
    Anchorage

Arizona
  Heard Museum, Phoenix
  Phoenix Art Museum
  Tucson Museum of Art
  University of Arizona Museum
    of Art, Tucson

Arkansas
  Arkansas Arts Center, Little
    Rock

California
  Crocker Museum of Art, Sacra-
    mento
  de Saisset Gallery and Museum,
    University of Santa Clara
  Edward-Dean Museum of Dec-
    orative Art, Cherry Valley
  Fine Arts Museums of San Fran-
    cisco
  J. Paul Getty Museum, Malibu
  La Jolla Museum of Contempo-
    rary Arts
  Long Beach Museum of Art
  Los Angeles Center for Photo-
    graphic Studies

Los Angeles County Museum of Art

Mingei International Museum of World Folk Art

Monterey Peninsula Museum of Art

Newport Harbor Art Museum, Newport Beach

Oakland Museum

Palm Springs Desert Museum

San Diego Museum of Art

San Francisco Museum of Art

Santa Barbara Museum of Art

University Art Museum, California State University, Long Beach

University Art Museum, University of California, Berkeley

University Art Museum, University of California, Santa Barbara

Wight Art Gallery, University of California, Los Angeles

Colorado

Denver Museum of Art

Museum of Western Art, Denver

Connecticut

Connecticut Historical Society, Hartford

Lyman Allan Museum, New London

Wadsworth Atheneum, Hartford

William Benton Museum of Art, University of Connecticut, Storrs

Yale University Art Museum, New Haven

Delaware

Delaware Art Museum, Wilmington

Henry Francis du Pont Winterthur Museum, Winterthur

District of Columbia

Corcoran Gallery of Art

Daughters of the American Revolution Museum

Hirshhorn Museum and Sculpture Garden

National Gallery of Art

Renwick Gallery, National Museum of American Art

Smithsonian Institution

Textile Museum

Florida

Bass Museum of Art, Miami Beach

Cornell Fine Arts Center, Rollins College, Winter Park

Cummer Gallery of Art, Jacksonville

Henry Morrison Flagler Museum, Palm Beach

Jacksonville Art Museum

Lowe Art Museum, University of Miami, Coral Gables

111

Norton Gallery and School of Art, West Palm Beach
Society of the Four Arts Museum, Palm Beach

Georgia
Atlanta Historical Society Museum
Columbus Museum of Arts and Science
Georgia Museum of Art, University of Georgia, Athens
High Museum of Art, Atlanta
Telfair Academy of Arts and Sciences, Savannah

Hawaii
Honolulu Academy of Arts

Idaho
Boise Gallery
Idaho State Historical Museum, Boise

Illinois
Art Institute of Chicago
Illinois State Museum, Springfield
Krannert Art Museum, University of Illinois, Champaign
Museum of Contemporary Art, Chicago

Indiana
Ball State University Art Gallery, Muncie

Evansville Museum of Art and Sciences
Indiana University Art Museum, Bloomington
Indianapolis Museum of Art
Sheldon Swope Art Gallery, Terre Haute

Iowa
Blanden Memorial Art Gallery, Fort Dodge
Brunnier Gallery and Museum, Iowa State University, Ames
Cedar Rapids Museum of Art
Museum of Art, University of Iowa, Iowa City
University of Northern Iowa Museum, Cedar Falls

Kansas
Spencer Museum of Art, University of Kansas, Lawrence
Wichita Art Museum

Kentucky
J. B. Speed Art Museum, Louisville
University of Kentucky Art Museum, Lexington

Louisiana
Historic New Orleans Collection
Louisiana State Museum, New Orleans
Magnolia Mound Plantation, Baton Rouge

Meadows Museum of Art, Centenary College of Louisiana, Shreveport

New Orleans Museum of Art

Maine

Bowdoin College Museum of Art, Brunswick

Brick Store Museum, Kennebunk

Portland Museum of Art

William A. Farnsworth Library and Art Museum, Rockland

Maryland

Art Gallery, University of Maryland, College Park

Baltimore Museum of Art

Walters Art Gallery, Baltimore

Washington County Museum of Fine Arts, Hagerstown

Massachusetts

Fogg Art Museum, Harvard University, Cambridge

Hancock Shaker Village, Pittsfield

Harrison Grey Otis House, Society for the Preservation of New England Antiquities, Boston

Heritage Plantation of Sandwich

Isabella Stewart Gardner Museum, Boston

Mead Art Museum, Amherst

Museum of American Textile History, Andover

Museum of Fine Arts, Boston

Old Sturbridge Village

Paul Revere House, Boston

Peabody Museum of Salem

Pilgrim Hall, Plymouth

Sandwich Glass Museum

Sterling and Francine Clark Art Institute, Williamstown

Worcester Art Museum

Michigan

Cranbrook Academy of Art, Bloomfield Hills

Detroit Institute of Arts

Ella Sharp Museum, Jackson

Flint Institute of Arts

Grand Rapids Art Museum

Henry Ford Museum and Greenfield Village, Dearborn

Krasl Art Center, St. Joseph

Kresge Art Museum, Michigan State University, East Lansing

Saginaw Art Museum

University of Michigan Art Museum, Ann Arbor

Minnesota

Minneapolis Institute of Arts

Minnesota Museum of Art, St. Paul

Walker Art Center, Minneapolis

Mississippi

Lauren Rogers Art Museum, Laurel

Manship House, Jackson

State Historical Museum, Jackson

University Museums, University of Mississippi, University

Missouri

Albrecht Art Museum, St. Joseph

Kansas City Museum

Laumeier Sculpture Garden, St. Louis

Museum of Art and Archaeology, University of Missouri, Columbia

Nelson-Atkins Museum of Art, Kansas City

St. Louis Art Museum

Montana

C. M. Russell Museum, Great Falls

Yellowstone Art Center, Billings

Nebraska

Joslyn Art Museum, Omaha

Sheldon Memorial Art Gallery, University of Nebraska, Lincoln

Thomas P. Kennard House, Nebraska State Historical Society, Lincoln

Nevada

Lost City Museum, Overton

Sierra Nevada Museum of Art, Reno

Wilbur D. May Museum, Reno

New Hampshire

Currier Gallery of Art, Manchester

Governor John Langdon Memorial Mansion, Society for the Preservation of New England Antiquities, Portsmouth

Hood Museum, Dartmouth College, Hanover

New Hampshire Historical Society Museum, Concord

Strawbery Banke, Portsmouth

New Jersey

Monmouth County Historical Association, Freehold

Montclair Art Museum

Museum of Art, Princeton University

Newark Museum

New Jersey Historical Association, Newark

New Jersey State Museum, Trenton

New Mexico

Albuquerque Museum

Institute of American Indian Arts Museum, Santa Fe

Museum of International Folk Art, Santa Fe

Museum of New Mexico, Santa Fe

Philmont Museums, Cimarron

Roswell Museum and Art Center

New York

Albany Institute of History and Art

Albright-Knox Art Gallery, Buffalo

American Craft Museum, New York

Arnot Art Museum, Elmira

Brooklyn Museum

Corning Museum of Glass

Everson Museum of Art, Syracuse

Frick Collection, New York

Herbert F. Johnson Museum of Art, Cornell University, Ithaca

Hudson River Museum, Yonkers

Hyde Collection, Glens Falls

International Center for Photography, New York

Jewish Museum, New York

Memorial Art Gallery, University of Rochester

Metropolitan Museum of Art, New York

Museum of Art, Munson-Williams-Proctor Institute, Utica

Museum of the American Indian, New York

Museum of the American Numismatic Society, New York

Museum of the City of New York

Museum of Modern Art, New York

National Academy of Design Museum, New York

New-York Historical Society Museum

Parrish Art Museum, Southampton

Picker Art Gallery, Colgate University, Hamilton

Pierpont Morgan Library, New York

Remington Art Museum, Ogdensburg

Shaker Museum Foundation, Old Chatham

Solomon R. Guggenheim Museum of Art, New York

Studio Museum in Harlem, New York

Whitney Museum of American Art, New York

North Carolina

Ackland Art Museum, University of North Carolina, Chapel Hill

Asheville Art Museum

Duke University Art Museum, Durham

Greenville Museum of Art

Museum of Early Southern Decorative Arts, Winston-Salem

North Carolina Museum of Art, Raleigh

St. John's Museum of Art, Wilmington

Ohio

Akron Art Museum
Allen Memorial Art Museum, Oberlin College
Canton Art Institute
Cincinnati Museum of Art
Cleveland Museum of Art
Columbus Museum of Art
Dayton Art Institute
Miami University Art Museum, Oxford
Ohio Historical Society Museum, Columbus
Springfield Art Center
Taft Museum, Cincinnati
Toledo Museum of Art

Oklahoma

Museum of Art, University of Oklahoma, Norman
Oklahoma Art Center, Oklahoma City
Philbrook Art Center, Tulsa
Thomas Gilcrease Institute of American History and Art, Tulsa

Oregon

Museum of Art, University of Oregon, Eugene
Portland Art Museum

Pennsylvania

Allentown Art Museum
Brandywine River Museum, Chadds Ford

Carnegie Mellon Museum of Art, Pittsburgh
Museum of the University of Pennsylvania, Philadelphia
Pennsylvania Academy of Fine Art, Philadelphia
Philadelphia Museum of Art and Rodin Museum
Woodmere Art Museum, Philadelphia

Rhode Island

Museum of Art, Rhode Island School of Design, Providence

South Carolina

Columbia Museum
Gibbes Art Gallery, Charleston
Greenville County Museum of Art
McKissick Museums, University of South Carolina, Columbia

South Dakota

South Dakota Memorial Art Museum, Brookings

Tennessee

Carroll Reece Museum, East Tennessee State University, Johnson City
Dixon Gallery and Gardens, Memphis
Hunter Museum of Art, Chattanooga

Memphis Brooks Memorial Art Gallery

Texas

Amarillo Art Center
Amon Carter Museum of Western Art, Fort Worth
Archer M. Huntington Art Gallery, University of Texas, Austin
Art Museum of South Texas, Corpus Christi
Contemporary Arts Museum, Houston
Dallas Museum of Art
El Paso Museum
Fort Worth Art Museum
Kimbell Art Museum, Fort Worth
Marion Koogler McNay Art Institute, San Antonio
McAllen International Museum
Museum of Fine Arts, Houston
Tyler Museum of Art

Utah

Utah Museum of Fine Arts, University of Utah, Salt Lake City

Vermont

Bennington Museum, Old Bennington
Shelburne Museum

Virginia

Abby Aldrich Rockefeller Folk Art Center, Colonial Wil-

liamsburg Foundation
Chrysler Museum, Norfolk
Colonial Williamsburg, Colonial Williamsburg Foundation
Roanoke Museum of Fine Arts
Valentine Museum, Richmond
Virginia Museum of Fine Arts, Richmond

Washington

Henry Art Gallery, University of Washington, Seattle
Seattle Art Museum
Tacoma Art Museum

West Virginia

Huntington Museum of Art
Oglebay Institute–Mansion Museum, Wheeling

Wisconsin

Bergstrom-Mahler Museum, Neenah
Charles A. Wustum Museum of Fine Arts, Racine
Elevehjam Art Center, University of Wisconsin, Madison
John Michael Kohler Arts Center, Sheboygan
Madison Art Center
Milwaukee Art Museum
Paine Art Center and Arboretum, Oshkosh

Wyoming

University of Wyoming Art Museum, Laramie

117

*P*roduct Sources

■

The following products are available from dealers in conservation supplies (see list starting on page 120).

acid-free board
acid-free boxes
acid-free paper
acid-free tissue paper
air purification systems
alkaline tissue paper
all-rag board
archival book covers
archival boxes
archival photograph albums
archival portfolios
Denglas
display boxes for valued objects
Filmoplast 90 acid-free pressure-
  sensitive tape
Gore-Tex
Granny's Old-fashioned Stain Re-
  mover
Incralac
leather dressing for books
light-measuring devices
lignin-free boxes

microcrystalline paste wax
museum board
Mylar cover sheets for photographs
neutral tissue paper
orthophenylphenol crystals
Orvis WA Paste
polyester clear film
polyethylene cover sheets for
  photographs
polyethylene sheets
polypropylene
polypropylene cover sheets for
  photographs
process board
relative-humidity measuring devices
Renaissance Wax
solander boxes
thymol cabinets
thymol crystals
triacetate covers for photographs
Tyvek covers for photographs

The following products are available from paint or hardware stores.

beeswax
calcium carbonate
DDVP (diethyldichlorovinylphos-
  phate)
dry-cleaning solvents

felt disks and pads
Goddard's Silver Polish
Incralac
linseed oil
no-pest strips

oxalic acid
paracrystals
paranuggets
PDB (paradichlorobenzene)
petroleum solvents
precipitated chalk

rottenstone
sodium hexametaphosphate
turpentine
whiting
Whink
Zenith Tibet Almond Stick

The following products are available from drugstores or pharmacies:

calcium carbonate
camphor oil
cotton swabs
denatured alcohol
diatomaceous earth

glycerin
peppermint oil
petroleum jelly
rubbing alcohol

The following products are available from grocery stores:

chlorine bleach
cornmeal
cornstarch
Ensure
Fels Naptha
hydrogen peroxide for bleaching
hydrogen peroxide 3 percent
Ivory Soap

lemon oil
Lestoil
Lysol Spray
Murphy Oil Soap
peroxy all-fabric bleach
sizing spray
steel wool

The following products are available from glass stores:

Denglas
Lucite

Permacryl
Plexiglas

The following products are available from sources as indicated:

fur hangers—furrier or fur supply store
ham for ironing—dry-cleaner supply store
jeweler's rouge—jewelers's supply store
muslin clothing bags—department store
padded hangers—department store
photographic light meters—photography equipment store

Conservation Supplies

■

Conservation Materials, Ltd.
240 Freeport Blvd.
Sparks, NV 89431
(702) 331-0582
All conservation supplies.

Conservation Resources International, Inc.
8000-H Forbes Place
Springfield, VA 22151
(703) 321-7730
Archival storage supplies for paper, prints, negatives; UV shields, polyester dealing machines, polyester envelopes.

Frank B. Ross Co., Inc.
22 Halladay St.
Jersey City, NJ 07304
(201) 433-3512
Custom-made waxes.

Franklin Distributors Corp.
P.O. Box 320
Denville, NJ 07834
(201) 267-2710
Archival filing systems for slides, prints, negatives, and documents.

The Hollinger Corporation
1810 S. Four Mile Run Dr.

Arlington, VA 22206
(703) 671-6600
All archival supplies.

Light Impressions Corporation
439 Monroe Ave.
Rochester, NY 14607
(716) 271-8960
(800) 823-6216
Archival display and storage systems; rag board; acid-free portfolios; Denglas; exhibition traveling crates; encapsulation materials, adhesives.

Museum Services Corporation
226 Hoard Ave.
Kensington, MD 20895
(301) 564-1225
Machinery for conservation of paintings, prints, drawings, textiles; shipping crates; support panels for relining and consolidation of paintings, prints, textiles; shadow boxes, frames and display cases; supplies for wood and paper.

Nielsen & Bainbridge
40 Eisenhower Dr.
Paramus, NJ 07653
(201) 368-9191
Mat, illustration, art, and mu-

seum board; all supplies for framing and for conservation.

Photofile
2000 Lewis Ave.
Zion, IL 60099
(312) 872-7557
All archival supplies.

Process Materials Company
301 Veterans Blvd.
Rutherford, NJ 07070
(201) 935-2900
Specialty products for restoration, conservation, and storage of museum and library materials.

Strobelite Co., Inc.
430 W. 14th St.
New York, NY 10014
(212) 929-3778
UV blacklight lamps for detecting restorations on art objects and inspecting removal of old varnish.

TALAS, Division of Technical Library Service, Inc.
213 W. 35th St.
New York, NY 10001
(212) 736-7744
All archival conservation and storage supplies; bookbinding, photographic, textile, and library supplies.

Transilwrap Company, Inc.
2615 N. Paulina

Chicago, IL 60614
(312) 528-8000
Archival storage, laminating, and dry-mounting materials.

University Products, Inc.
517 Main St.
Holyoke, MA 01040
(413) 532-9431
(800) 628-1912
Archival storage and display materials for conservation, restoration, and preservation.

Books and Papers

■

Aiko's Art Material Import, Inc.
714 N. Wabash Ave.
Chicago, IL 60611
(312) 943-0745
Handmade Japan paper; all materials for preserving and restoring fine arts.

Andrews/Nelson/Whitehead
31-10 48th Ave.
Long Island City, NY 11101
(718) 937-7100
Papers and board for conservation and restoration.

APF Kulicke
783 Madison Ave.
New York, NY 10021

(212) 988-1090
Frames designed for display of fragile and valuable paper objects.

Applied Science Labs, Inc.
2216 Hull St.
Richmond, VA 23224
(804) 231-9386
Try-test and format spot testing paper kits for stability testing of paper, books, and documents; chemical analysis of paper, books, and documents.

Crestwood Paper Co., Inc.
315 Hudson St.
New York, NY 10013
(212) 989-2700
Handmade, mold-made, and machine-made papers and boards for the fine arts.

Fox River Paper Company
200 E. Washington St.
Suite 300
Appleton, WI 54913
(414) 733-7341
Archival papers.

Interleaf, Inc.
212 Second St. N
Minneapolis, MN 55401
(612) 332-1313
Vapor phase deacidification to preserve materials that are being destroyed from acids in paper.

Micro Essential Laboratory, Inc.
4224 Ave. H
Brooklyn, NY 11210
(718) 338-3618
Archivist pH pencils; humidicator paper for estimation of humidity; pH test papers.

Miller Cardboard
75 Wooster St.
New York, NY 10012
(212) 226-0833
Acid-free and all-rag museum mounting boards; acid-free barrier paper.

Mohawk Paper Mills, Inc.
465 S. Saratoga St.
Cohoes, NY 12047
(518) 237-1740
Acid-free papers.

Parks & Stock, Inc.
67 W. 73rd St.
New York, NY 10023
(212) 877-2480
Storage, framing, and display for archival products.

Rising Paper Company
Park St.
Housatonic, MA 01236
(413) 274-3345
Printing and writing papers, artist's papers, museum boards.

Somerville Gallery
167 E. 87th St.
New York, NY 10128
(212) 427-4333
Frames for display of valuable and fragile paper objects.

TALAS, Division of Technical Library Service, Inc.
213 W. 35th St.
New York, NY 10001
(212) 736-7744
All supplies for books and paper.

Wei T'o Associates, Inc.
21750 Main St., #27
Matteson, IL 60443
(312) 747-6660
Nonaqueous deacidification solution and sprays and application equipment; disaster recovery, freeze-drying and nonchemical fumigation equipment; library and museum paper artifacts.

Environmental Monitoring and Control

■

Abbecon-Cal, Inc.
123 Gray Ave.
Santa Barbara, CA 93101
(805) 966-0810
Humidity indicators and recorders; technical instruments.

Airguide Instrument Co.
2210 Wabansia Ave.
Chicago, IL 60647
(312) 486-3000
Barometers, thermometers, humidity indicators.

Applied Science Labs, Inc.
2216 Hull St.
Richmond, VA 23224
(804) 231-9386
Pollution-control supplies.

Beckman Industrial Corp., Cedar Grove Division
89 Commerce Rd.
Cedar Grove, NJ 07009
(201) 239-6200
Moisture and relative humidity instrumentation and systems.

Belfort Instrument Co.
727 S. Wolf St.
Baltimore, MD 21231
(301) 342-2626
Hygro thermograph for temperature and humidity recording.

Humidial Corporation
465 N. Mt. Vernon Ave.
Colton, CA 92324
(714) 825-1793
Humidity indicators; dehydrators, moisture indicators.

Johnson Controls, Inc.
  507 E. Michigan St.
  Milwaukee, WI 53201
  (414) 274-4000
  Building automation systems for temperature, humidity, and fire-safety control.

Laboratory Supplies Co., Inc.
  29 Jefry Lane
  Hicksville, NY 11801
  (516) 681-7711
  Environment measurement instruments.

Micro Essential Laboratory, Inc.
  4224 Ave. H
  Brooklyn, NY 11210
  (718) 338-3618
  Humidicator paper for estimation of humidity; pH test papers.

Multiform Desiccant Products, Inc.
  1418 Niagara St.
  Buffalo, NY 14213
  (716) 883-8900
  Silica gel.

Newport Scientific, Inc.
  8246 E. Sandy Court
  Jessup, MD 20794
  (301) 498-6700
  Humidity measuring and control instruments; superpressure line and hygrodynamics.

Phys-Chemical Research Corp.
  36 W. 20th St.
  New York, NY 10011
  (212) 924-2070
  Relative humidity sensors and instruments.

Qualimetrics, Inc.
  1165 National Dr.
  Sacramento, CA 95834
  (916) 923-0055
  Environmental monitoring equipment.

Research Products Corporation
  1015 E. Washington Ave.
  Madison, WI 53701
  (608) 257-8801
  Humidifiers, nonelectronic air cleaners.

Science Associates, Inc.
  11 State Rd.
  Princeton, NJ 08540
  (609) 924-4470
  UV monitors; temperature and humidity indicators, recorders, controllers, and alarms.

Skuttle Manufacturing Company
  Rte. 1
  Marietta, OH 45750
  (614) 373-9169
  Humidifiers, humidistats, hygrometers, humidifier water treatment, make-up air control, air filters.

Stultz America, Inc.
270 Technology Park
5310 Spectrum Dr., Suite H
Frederick, MD 21701
(301) 663-8885
Ultrasonic humidification products designed to use deionized water.

United States Gypsum Company
101 S. Wacker Dr.
Chicago, IL 60606
(312) 321-3863
Soluble anhydrite as a desiccant for humidity control.

Wahl Instruments, Inc.
5750 Hannum Ave.
Culver City, CA 90231
(213) 641-6931
Temperature measurement instruments.

Walton Laboratories
1 Carol Place
Moonachie, NJ 07074
(201) 641-5700
Humidification products.

Watrous & Company, Inc.
P.O. Box 996
Cutchogue, NY 11935
(516) 734-5504
Instruments for monitoring the atmosphere; hygrometers, barometers, thermometers; recording and control instruments.

Yellow Springs Instrument Co.
Box 279
Yellow Springs, OH 45387
(513) 767-7241
Temperature and humidity measurement and control system.

Fumigation Equipment

■

Environmental Tectonics Corporation
County Line Industrial Park
Southampton, PA 18966
(215) 355-9100
Fumigation equipment.

Sanitized, Inc.
605 Third Ave.
New York, NY 10158
(212) 867-0033
Antibacterial and antifungal preservative chemicals.

Vacudyne, Inc.
375 E. Joe Orr Rd.
Chicago Heights, IL 60411
(312) 757-5200
Fumigation systems for artifacts and books.

Light Filtering and Monitoring Equipment

■

Duro-Test Corporation
2321 Kennedy Blvd.
North Bergen, NJ 07047
(201) 867-7000
Special-purpose bulbs.

International Light Company
Dexeter Industrial Green
Newburyport, MA 01950
(617) 465-5923
Photometers for measurement of visible and ultraviolet light.

Lighting Services, Inc.
158 E. 58th St.
New York, NY 10155
(212) 838-8633
Museum lighting equipment.

Plastic-View International, Inc.
15468 Cabrito Rd.
Van Nuys, CA 91409
(818) 786-2801
Nonglare shades; solar-control window film for reducing heat, glare, and ultraviolet radiation.

Solar-Screen Company
53-11 105th St.
Corona, NY 11368
(718) 592-8222
Filtering shades, film, fluorescent shades, light-reflective materials.

Verilux, Inc.
35 Mason St.
Greenwich, CT 06830
(203) 869-3750
Color-balanced, low-ultraviolet-emission fluorescent tubes.

West Lake Plastic Company
West Lenni Rd.
Lenni Mills, PA 19052
(215) 459-1000
Rigid plastic ultraviolet filter tubes for fluorescent lights.

Bibliography

■

Andre, Jean-Michel. *The Restorers Handbook of Ceramics and Glass.* New York: Van Nostrand Reinhold Co., 1976.

Barclay, R., R. Eames, and A. Todd. *The Care of Wooden Objects.* Ottawa: Canadian Conservation Institute, June 1983.

Beecher, Miss. *Miss Beecher's Housekeeper and Healthkeeper.* New York, Harper & Brothers, 1873.

Beeton, Isabella. *Mrs. Beeton's Book of Household Management.* Rev. ed. London: Chancellor Press, 1982. First published 1859.

Brewer, Darlyn. "Giving an Old Pot a Brand New Lining." *The New York Times,* October 1, 1987.

Browning, B. L. "The Nature of Paper." In *Deterioration and Preservation of Library Materials,* H. W. Winger and R. D. Smith, eds. Chicago: University of Chicago Press, 1970.

Clapp, Anne F. *Curatorial Care of Works of Art on Paper.* Oberlin, Ohio: Intermuseum Conservation Association, 1978.

The Cleaning, Polishing and Protective Waxing of Brass and Copper Objects. Ottawa: Canadian Conservation Institute, June 1978.

Collins, Glenn. "Fading Memories: Albums Damage Photos." *The New York Times,* October 3, 1987. Style Section.

"Conservation of the Decorative Arts." Washington, D.C.: American Association of Museums, *Museum News,* 1976–77.

Conservation of Photographs. Rochester, N.Y.: Eastman Kodak, 1985.

DeWitt, Donald L., and Carol Burlinson. "Leather Bookbindings: Preservation Techniques." Nashville, Tenn.: American Association for State and Local History, *History News* 32:8 (August 1977).

Dolloff, Francis W., and Roy L. Perkinson. *How to Care for Works of Art on Paper.* 4th ed. Boston: Museum of Fine Arts, 1985.

Fales, Mrs. Dean A., Jr. "The Care of Antique Silver." Technical Leaflet No. 40. Nashville: The American Association for State and Local History, 1967.

Feller, Robert L. "Control of Deteriorating Effects of Light on Museum Objects." Washington, D.C.: American Association of Museums, *Museum News*, May 1968.

Finch, Karen, and Greta Putnam. *Caring for Textiles.* New York: Watson-Guptill Publications, 1977.

Florman, Monte, ed. *How to Clean Practically Anything.* Mount Vernon, N.Y.: Consumers Union, 1986.

Gulbeck, Per E. *The Care of Antiques and Historical Collections.* 2nd ed. Bruce A. MacLeish rev. Nashville: American Association for State and Local History Press, 1985.

Horton, Carolyn. *Cleaning and Preserving Bindings and Related Materials.* Chicago: American Library Association, 1979.

Housekeeping Our Heritage: Practical Advice for Alberta Collections. Edmonton: Provincial Museum of Alberta, 1984.

Keck, Caroline K. *How To Take Care of Your Paintings.* New York: Charles Scribner's Sons, 1978.

"Matting Works on Paper." Ottawa: Canadian Observation Institute, April 1986.

Mayer, Ralph. *The Artist's Handbook of Materials and Techniques.* 3rd ed. New York: Viking Press, 1980.

McGriffin, Robert F. *Basic Furniture Care.* Waterford: New York State Office of Parks and Recreation, Division for Historic Preservation, 1980.

Merrill, William. "Wood Deterioration: Causes and Prevention." Technical Leaflet 77. Nashville, Tenn.: American Association for State and Local History, 1974.

Moore, Alma Chestnut. *How to Clean Everything.* 3rd ed. New York: Simon & Schuster, 1977.

Moore, N. Hudson. *Old Pewter, Brass, Copper and Sheffield Plate.* Rutland, Vt.: Charles E. Tuttle Co., 1972.

Myers, G. M. "Rugs: Preservation, Display and Storage." Washington, D.C.: American Association of Museums, *Museum News*, June 1952.

Perkinson, Roy L. "Conserving Works of Art on Paper." Washington, D.C.: American Association of Museums, 1977.

"Protective Enclosures for Books and Paper Artifacts." Ottawa: Canadian Conservation Institute, September 1983.

Rinzler, Carol Ann. *The Consumer's Brand-Name Guide to Household Products.* New York: Lippincott & Crowell, 1980.

Rowlinson, Eric B. "Rules for Handling Works of Art." Washington, D.C.: American Association of Museums, *Museum News*, April 1975.

Sandwith, Hermione, and Sheila Stanton. *The National Trust Manual of Housekeeping.* London: Penguin Books, in Association with the National Trust, 1984.

Stange, Eric. "Millions of Books Are Turning to Dust—Can They Be Saved?" *The New York Times Book Review*, March 29, 1987.

"Storing Works on Paper." Ottawa: Canadian Conservation Institute, April 1986.

Thomson, Garry. *The Museum Environment.* Woburn, Mass.: Butterworth, 1978.

Tomkins, Calvin. "Profiles: Colored Muds in a Sticky Substance." *The New Yorker*, March 16, 1987.

Varese, Michael. "Protecting Furniture's Finish." *The New York Times*, October 1, 1987.

———. "Restoring the Luster of Brass Hardware." *The New York Times*, October 22, 1987.

Watson, Edwin W. "Oriental Carpets: Selection, Use and Care." Nashville, Tenn.: American Association for State and Local History, *History News* 34:12 (December 1979).

Acknowledgments

■

We are grateful to many institutions and individuals who gave us direction and provided information for this book. Among them, we would especially like to thank Barbara Barber, Nina Bourne, Lily Cates, I. J. Chiarello, Janet Dobson, William Doyle, Ralph O. Esmerian, Maria Tucci Gottlieb, Elaine Haas, Donald Moore, the Museum of American Folk Art, Nello Nanni, Carolyn Niezgoda, Helene von Rosenstiel, Ned Sarasi, Ray Somerville, TALAS (Technical Library Service), O. C. Taylor, and Joel Zakow.

We are indebted to our agent, Mary Yost, for her encouragement, support, and sense of humor.

*I*ndex

∎